The General Educator's Guide to Special Education

A Resource Handbook for all who Work with Children with Special Needs

Jody L Maanum

Peytral Publications, Inc.
Minnetonka, MN   55345

Publisher's Cataloging-in-Publication
(Provided by Quality Books, Inc.)

Maanum, Jody L.
    The general educator's guide to special education : a resource handbook for all
who work with children with special needs / Jody L. Maanum.--1st edition
    p. cm.
    Includes bibliographical references and index.
    Audience: K-12 educators
    1-890455-32-6

    1. Special education--Handbooks, manuals, etc.
  2. Special education--United States--Handbooks, manuals
etc. I. Title

    LC3965.M33 2001   371.9'0973
                                QBI01-700582

Library of Congress   2001   132434

10 9 8 7 6 5 4 3 2
Printed in the United States of America

Published by:
Peytral Publications, Inc.
PO Box 1162
Minnetonka, MN 55345-0162
Tel: 1 877-PEYTRAL (739-8725)
www.peytral.com

Table of Contents

Section II

Section III

Section IV

Section V

Acknowledgements

I would like to thank Deanne Borgeson, for willingly leading my committee and for advising, supporting, and assisting me through the final phase of my Master's program. She is my mentor.

To Linda Svobodny, Brian Smith and John Benson, members of my committee for understanding the need for and allowing me to create this resource.

To Heidi Krause, my colleague and friend, for her countless hours of reading and re-reading this resource in an attempt to keep me focused.

To Dr. Thelma Anderson, my amazing grandma, for her grammatical expertise and words of praise and encouragement. I will always look to her with admiration.

To all of my students – past, present, and future – who have and continue to teach, motivate, and challenge me to be the best I can be.

To my parents, siblings, and family for their love, patience, and never-ending encouragement. I am blessed with you, my family.

Finally, to my husband and best friend, Joel, and daughter, Lacee Jo, for their confidence, support, encouragement, and patience throughout this entire process. This accomplishment became reality because of you.

Section I

Definitions of Special Education Disability Categories

Special Education Disability Categories

The Federal Guidelines for Special Education recognizes 15 different disability categories in which students may be determined eligible to receive special education and related services. A student must meet specified criteria prior to being deemed eligible to receive special education and related services.

The 15 qualifying categories are:

1. **Autism**
2. **Deaf-Blindness**
3. **Developmental Adapted Physical Education: Special Education (DAPE)**
4. **Early Childhood Special Education (ECSE)**
5. **Emotional or Behavioral Disorders (E/BD)**
6. **Hearing Impairment (HI)**
7. **Mild-Moderate Mentally Impaired (MMMI)**
8. **Moderate-Severe Mentally Impaired (MSMI)**
9. **Other Health Impaired (OHI)**
10. **Physically Impaired**
11. **Severely Multiply Impaired**
12. **Specific Learning Disabilities (SLD)**
13. **Speech or Language Impairment**
14. **Traumatic Brain Injury (TBI)**
15. **Visually Impaired (VI)**

On the following pages, you will find definitions of the 15 disability categories. Specific examples of medical conditions, which would fall within these categories as well as possible educational approaches to working with children placed in these categories, will also be provided where appropriate.

1. Autism

Autism is a developmental disability that affects a child's verbal and non-verbal communication skills as well as a child's ability to appropriately interact in social situations. This condition affects approximately 1 in 2000 births. The cause of Autism is not clear; however, it is thought to have a biological basis. Autism is a lifelong disability with onset usually prior to 30 months of age. It does occur on a continuum from mild to severe and can occur by itself or in association with cognitive disorders such as mental retardation or learning disabilities. Asperger's Syndrome is in the continuum of Autism and has been called the "mild" form of autism.

Characteristics of Autism.

There are six frequently observed characteristics of children with autism.

1) **Apparent sensory deficit**
   Children with autism often appear to not see or hear things that are directed toward them. Even when the proximity is directly in front of the child, the child still may not react as if anyone is communicating with him or her.

2) **Severe affect isolation.**
   This is noticed when someone attempts to love, cuddle, or show affection to the child. The child may respond with profound lack of interest and will often push away from that attempt of affection.

3) **Self-Stimulation.**
   Children with autism will often exhibit repetitive stereotyped acts, such as rocking when in a sitting or standing position, twirling around (often on tip toes), flapping hands, or humming a tune over and over again. They often become engrossed in staring at lights or spinning objects that seem to capture their attention.

4) **Tantrums and self-mutilatory behavior.**
   It is noted that often times children with autism may bite themselves until the bite causes blood, or will beat their heads against walls or furniture so hard that large lumps or bruises appear on the skin. A child may beat his or her face with fists, or even direct his or her aggression outward toward others by biting, kicking, and scratching. Once a child begins such a rage, it is difficult for parents or other adults to know how to handle and cope with these behaviors.

5) **Echolalic and psychotic speech.**
   Many autistic children are mute, meaning they do not speak words or communicable language, but they may hum or utter simple sounds. Sometimes the speech of those who do talk will just echo that of what other people are saying to them. For example when a child is asked "What is your name?" the child may

respond with "What is your name?" Sometimes the echolalia (echoing someone else's words) are not immediate, but delayed. The child may repeat things heard, like TV commercials or other information that he or she has heard prior to that time.

6) Behavior deficiencies.

Along with the behaviors described above, there are many behaviors that are not exhibited by an autistic child, that should be. By the age of 5 or 10, autistic children may show behavioral abilities of a 1-year-old child. They often exhibit few to no self-help skills, and need to be fed and dressed by others. These children often show no understanding or fear of common dangers.

Educational approaches for Autism

Children with autism require and strive from structure and consistent scheduling. This helps the child to understand what will be happening and coming up. This will also help the child to remain calm and not become as easily upset and agitated when schedules change. Structure and schedules that are followed consistently help the child to learn better as well as to become more independent.

Physical Structure is the way that we set up and organize each area in our classroom. A child with autism needs clear physical and visual boundaries so he or she knows where each area begins and ends. Minimizing visual and auditory distractions is also important to help this child focus on learning concepts and not irrelevant details. The child also needs to know the basic teaching areas of the room. There needs to be specific spots that the child goes to everyday for a snack, play time, transition times, as well as individual and independent work times. These spots need to be consistent everyday so there are no "surprises". If a child with autism is used to having a snack on the carpeted area at the front of the room everyday, and suddenly he or she is expected to eat a snack at his or her desk, this will likely cause agitation. Children with autism require consistency in all aspects of their day.

Daily Schedules are essential in visually telling the child with autism, in a way that he or she can understand, what activities will occur and in what order for that particular day. The child will work best if a concrete reference of the schedule is in view every day. This will help the child to better accept change and become a bit more flexible, as long as the child knows in advance of a schedule change. A fire drill, for example, may be a devastating addition to the day, if the child is unaware of it's occurrence. In the eyes of an autistic child, if that added event of the day is not written on the schedule, then that event should not happen. Helping the child to be aware of upcoming event changes will ensure easier transition times when those events occur.

Visual Structure helps children with autism to capitalize on their visual aptitude and strengths and minimize their deficits of auditory processing. Visually highlighting important information will help to clarify the relevant concepts of which the child should be aware. This may include color-coding areas and labeling things to visually draw a child's attention.   Providing visual instructions for the child is also helpful when presenting a child with an assignment or task.

It is important to remember that a child with autism needs consistency and structure. It is difficult for this child to be flexible without prior notice of a change in scheduling. If a child with autism does become upset, it is not because the child is being naughty or bad, it is often just that he or she was unaware of change and is unable to handle and cope with those changes like that of his or her age peers.

2. Deaf - Blindness

Deaf-Blindness is a medically verified visual impairment coexisting with a medically verified hearing impairment. Together, these impairments must cause severe communication difficulties and other developmental and educational problems that cannot be accommodated in special education programs solely for children with exclusive blindness or exclusive deafness.

3. Developmental Adapted Physical Education. Special Education (DAPE)

DAPE is specially designed physical education instruction and services for pupils with disabilities who have a substantial delay or disorder in physical development. Developmental Adapted Physical Education: Special Education (DAPE) instruction for pupils age three through 21 may include development of physical fitness, motor fitness, fundamental motor skill and patterns, skills in aquatics, dance, individual and group games, and sports.

Students with conditions such as obesity, temporary injuries, and short-term or temporary illness or disabilities are termed as special needs students. Special needs students **are not eligible** for Developmental Adapted Physical Education: Special Education. Provisions for these students must be made within regular physical education classes, rather than special education physical education classes.

If a child has been deemed eligible to receive special education services in the areas of autism, deaf-blindness, emotional or behavioral disabilities, hearing impaired, specific learning disabilities, mentally impaired, severely multiply impaired, other health impaired, physically impaired, visually impaired, or traumatic brain injury, and that child is unable to succeed in regular physical education class, that child **is eligible** to receive an adapted physical education class.

4. Early Childhood: Special Education (ECSE)

Early Childhood Special Education (ECSE) is to be made available to all children from birth to seven years of age who have a significant delay or disorder in development, or have an identifiable, medically diagnosed, sensory, physical, mental, or social/emotional condition or impairment known to hinder normal development.

The criteria for a child to be eligible for special education services in the area of Early Childhood Special Education states that the child must have a medically diagnosed syndrome or condition. Such medically diagnosed conditions may include, but are not limited to, the ones that are listed and described below.

Medically Diagnosed Syndromes

a. Cerebral Palsy (CP)

Cerebral Palsy is one of the most prevalent physical impairments in children. It is a long-term condition resulting from a lesion to the brain or an abnormality of brain growth. CP is a disorder in which muscular development and control are impaired. The significance of this injury and the effects vary for each person. The brain injury may occur prior to birth resulting from a disease or injury to the mother that affects the fetus, during a traumatic birth where there are complications, or later in life as the result of an infection, disease, or head trauma.

Obviously there is no cure for CP; however, it can be treated. The impairment usually does not get worse as a child ages. It is not fatal nor contagious. These children usually have disturbances of voluntary motor functions. This may include paralysis, extreme weakness, lack of coordination, involuntary convulsions, and other motor disorders. They may have little or no control over their arms, legs, or speech, depending on the degree of the impairment. It is possible to also have a hearing and/or vision impairment as well.

Educational approaches for Cerebral Palsy

The use of assistive technology and adaptive equipment can help a person with CP cope with some of the physical limitations due to this disability. Physical and occupational therapy will help to maintain good muscle quality. Some medication can be used to strengthen muscle groups as well. Speech therapy may be helpful if the muscles affecting speech are involved in the disability.

b. Chromosome Abnormalities

1. Down Syndrome

Down Syndrome is caused by the presence of an extra chromosome 21. It is very common and occurs in approximately one in 900 births. Children with Down Syndrome show some distinctive physical characteristics such as upwardly slanting eyes; small ear, nose, feet and hands; a flattened facial profile; short stature; a large tongue; and a gap between the first and second toes. Other results of this syndrome may be visual and auditory problems, thyroid disease, cardiac conditions, premature senility, loose ligaments, and decreased muscle tone. Due to low muscle tone, many people with Down Syndrome have a tendency to keep their mouths open. This problem of muscle tone coupled with a large tongue makes speech articulation more difficult. Mental retardation accompanies this syndrome but the level of intellectual ability varies. Most people with Down Syndrome function in the mild or moderate range of retardation. Cardiac problems are the major cause for concern of people with Down Syndrome.

Educational approaches for Down Syndrome

Down Syndrome is recognizable at birth, which allows for early intervention from a variety of professionals. Early intervention gives parents new information so they can help their child get a head start on learning. Typical professionals who can be involved in early intervention screening and follow-up are physicians, speech and language professionals, audiologists, education specialists, and physical and occupational therapists. A strength that is commonly noted about people with Down Syndrome is that they often have a pleasant disposition and behavior problems are uncommon.

2. Fragile X Syndrome

Fragile X Syndrome accounts for the most common inherited form of mental retardation. This syndrome is linked to an irregularity in the X chromosome and usually results in mental retardation in males and learning disorders in females. Physical characteristics of this syndrome include a prominent jaw, and a large head, ears, and testes in males. Behavioral concerns may be autistic-like behaviors such as withdrawal, heightened interest in sensations, stereotypical hand movements, behavior problems (hand biting), and hyperactivity.

Fragile X Syndrome is often difficult to diagnose as a child. The physical characteristics may be minimal or not noticed until they become more pronounced following puberty. There is a slow regression in abilities over time.

Educational approaches for Fragile X Syndrome

Early intervention is recommended so that physical therapy, speech and language therapy, and occupation therapy can be started. Positive behavioral strategies and medications have been used to improve problems of self injury and hyperactivity.

3. Hunter Syndrome

This condition is an X-linked syndrome that is genetically transmitted and affects only males but is carried by females. It is rare, as it occurs in approximately 1 in 50,000 births. Infants born with Hunter's Syndrome show no immediate outward signs. Normal or excessive growth within the first two years follows. The effects of Hunter's Syndrome become quite apparent after the second year of life. At this time there is observable mental deterioration that can result in aggressive and hyperactive behaviors. Typical physical characteristics will include small stature; short neck; joint contracture; large head (hydrocephalus); broad, low nose; full cheeks; thick lips; and wide spaced teeth. Impaired hearing usually begins later in childhood.

There are two types of Hunter's Syndrome: Type A and Type B. Type A is also called juvenile type and is the most severe. This type has rapid progression, severe mental retardation, and death before 15 years of age due to liver and cardiac problems. Type B progresses much more slowly. There is slight or no noticeable mental impairment and person's with Type B may live to be 50 or 60 years old.

Educational approaches for Hunter Syndrome

The interventions necessary for a child with Hunter Syndrome will depend on the type and severity of the symptoms. Early intervention is most helpful to address each individual's needs. Speech and language consultants can provide recommendations to enhance communication. Audiologists can assess and provide hearing devices for those with auditory problems. Surgery can be used to correct hernias and shunting can be implemented to decrease pressure on the brain. Behavior management consultants or psychologists can provide guidance in decreasing aggressive behaviors, increasing productive expression of wants and needs, and managing hyperactivity.

4. Klinefelter Syndrome (47XXY)

This genetic disorder develops in males only. It occurs in approximately 1 in every 500-1000 male births and is very common. This syndrome is caused by additional female X chromosomes on the chromosome chain that determines gender. This additional X chromosome affects the production of testosterone which can result in the following physical characteristics: small testes, lack of facial hair, and breast development.

Some common features of people with this syndrome are increased height, poor upper body strength, delay in language development, and difficulty with auditory processing. Mental retardation is not a prominent feature of this syndrome as only approximately 10-20% of the people with Klinefelter's have intelligence in the mild mental retardation or low normal range.

c. Fetal Alcohol Syndrome (FAS)

This syndrome is the leading cause of mental retardation and the second most common birth defect. It occurs in 1 in 600-700 births, and **is 100% preventable**. FAS is a condition characterized by physical and behavioral disabilities that occur because of exposure to alcohol prior to birth. The mother's use of alcohol during pregnancy is a criteria for diagnosis of these conditions. Other indications of this syndrome are small size; and distinctive facial features such as a small head; distinctive eye shape, size and position; flat nasal bridge; lack of crease between the nose and lip; thin upper lip; and a small jaw. Other physical problems such as joint and limb malformations, heart problems, kidney disorders and cleft lip/palate may be seen. Mental impairment is also a feature of this syndrome and can include mental retardation, learning disorders, behavior problems, and gross motor limitations.

Problems stemming from this disorder can be seen in infancy. Babies with FAS are usually born small and underdeveloped. Behavioral concerns may consist of hyperactivity, a short attention span, and decreased physical abilities are commonly noted in pre-school and school aged children.

Educational approaches for FAS

Early intervention does increase the child's chances for later success. Early intervention provides a variety of assessments in the areas of physical and mental ability. Physicians, physical and occupational therapists, speech and language therapists, and people who specialize in child development can assess the child's strengths and abilities along with areas where additional supports are needed. The best time for intervention to begin is shortly after birth.

d. Neural Tube defects

1. Spina Bifida

Spina Bifida is a disorder in which the spine has not sealed correctly around the spinal cord. An infant born with Spina Bifida has an opening on his or her backbone. This occurs in 1 in every 1000 to 2000 births. Some evidence does support that Spina Bifida is inherited. Researchers have also recently shown a link between diet and this disorder. It has been found that a small amount of the B vitamin, folic acid, taken the month prior to conception and during the first several months of pregnancy significantly reduces the chances of having a child with this birth defect.

There are three types of Spinal Bifida. The first is called Occulta and this is a harmless form. It is possible that people who have this never even know that they have Spina Bifida. In this form, there is a small gap in the vertebrae of the back. The spinal cord and nerves are not affected and no problems are caused by this gap.

The second and rarest type is called Meningocele. In this type, the protective membranes that surround the spine push out through an opening in the vertebrae creating a cyst. The cyst can be small or large. The spinal cord remains intact and the cyst is surgically removed. There is usually no subsequent damage and the child can go on to lead a life without further spinal complications.

The third type of Spina Bifida is the most complicated and severe. This type is called Myelomeningocele. This occurs when a portion of the spinal cord protrudes through the back. Often the cord is exposed and lacking spinal fluid. The cord may be covered with sores and is extremely prone to infection. Surgery is completed to seal up the opening, usually within the first 48 hours of life, but many complications still result. At the site of the exposed cord, and below, the child has paralysis. Because the nerves that control bowel and bladder functions are located very low on the spinal cord, 95% of people with this form of Spina Bifida will not have control of their bowel and bladder. Due to the damage to the spinal cord there are usually problems with the flow of spinal fluid from the brain which can result in a build up of fluid in the brain. This fluid can cause brain damage if not drained, so a shunting procedure is surgically performed to drain the excess fluid into other body cavities.

Educational approaches for Spina Bifida

Early intervention is important for a child with Spina Bifida. Physical therapists, occupational therapists, neurologists, neurosurgeons, orthopedists, pediatricians, nutritionists, psychologists, and nurses will be helpful to plan for and implement strategies to enable the person with this syndrome to be as comfortable and independent as possible. These children will usually walk with braces, crutches, or walkers, and they may use wheelchairs for longer distances.

e. Neuromuscular Disorders

1. Duchenne Muscular Dystrophy

This disorder is a progressive disease of muscle weakening and is the most common and severe form of childhood Muscular Dystrophy. It is genetically transmitted from the mother and affects only males. There are no physical characteristics of Duchenne's MD that make this syndrome noticeable at birth. A child with Duchenne's develops normally until the second to sixth year of life when the onset of this disease is first seen. Early symptoms such as falling, walking on toes, a protruding abdomen, and difficulty in running are often overlooked until more severe sign of this syndrome set in. There is a progressive weakening of the pelvis, upper arms, and upper legs. The use of a wheelchair may be required by age 12-15. Physical therapy can help people with Duchenne's MD prolong their ability to walk. In the later stages of Duchenne's the respiratory system is affected and breathing becomes difficult. This leads to an increase susceptibility to respiratory infections and pneumonia. Most people with Duchenne's MD have a life span of 20 - 30 years. Mental retardation is common with this syndrome.

Educational approaches for Muscular Dystrophy

People with MD will require support to maintain their physical health and independence. Intervention strategies include orthopedic support (wheelchairs, crutches, specialized beds), symptom treatment for infections, physical and occupational therapy to help maintain muscle conditions, and possible surgery for muscle contractures may be necessary. In school, a teacher should be careful not to lift a child with muscular dystrophy by the arms, as even a gentle pull may dislocate the child's limbs.

f. Cytomegalovirus (CMV)

Cytomegalovirus or CMV is a common virus in which most adults and children who come into contact with have no symptoms or problems. It is estimated, however, that approximately 1 percent of all newborns are infected with congenital CMV before birth, resulting in a serious disability in more than 4,000 children each year. In some cases children whose mothers were infected during pregnancy may have birth defects such as hearing loss, mental retardation, or delays in development.

Educational approaches for CMV

Specific educational planning will be made for children with this severe form of CMV.

g. Bronchopulmonary Dysplasia (BPD)

This is a chronic lung disease which those infected experience persistent difficulty in breathing and abnormal changes on chest X-rays. In most cases, BPD occurs in infants who are born prematurely and who have Respiratory Distress Syndrome (RDS). BPD most often surfaces after babies have required extra oxygen and/or a mechanical ventilator to treat their original lung problem. It is possible that the symptoms of BPD can disappear quite rapidly; however, some infants with BPD may have breathing difficulties for many months or years. Some infants may depend on a mechanical ventilator throughout early childhood. BPD survivors are at a higher risk of complications after the usual childhood infections. Babies who survive BPD tend to grow more slowly than normal. They usually remain smaller than normal children of the same age. Some may continue to have problems with lung function even when they are adults. The outlook for growth and development of babies with BPD varies. In severe cases, there may be some long-term limitations. These might include abnormalities in coordination, gait and muscle tone, inability to tolerate exercise, vision and hearing problems, and learning disabilities. For many, however, few complications are noticed after early childhood.

Educational approaches for BPD

For those children who exhibit limitations due to BPD when they reach school-age, special considerations will need to be taken regarding the physical expectation and requirements of this child.

5. Emotional or Behavioral Disorders (E/BD)

Emotional or Behavioral Disorders refer to an established pattern characterized by one or more of the following behavior clusters:

a. Severely aggressive or impulsive behaviors;
b. Severely withdrawn or anxious behaviors, general pervasive unhappiness, depression, or wide mood swings; or
c. Severely disordered thought processes manifested by unusual behavior patterns, atypical communication styles, and distorted interpersonal relationships.

This may include children with *schizophrenic disorders, affective disorders, anxiety disorders, or other sustained disorders of conduct or adjustment* when they adversely affect educational performance. The established pattern adversely affects educational performance and results in either 1) an inability to build or maintain satisfactory interpersonal relations necessary to the learning process with peers, teachers, and others, or 2) a failure to attain or maintain a satisfactory rate of educational or developmental progress that cannot be improved or explained by addressing intellectual, sensory, health, cultural, or linguistic factors. The established pattern of behavior needs to be noted that it is occurring to a marked degree and has been occurring for a long period of time.

The criteria for a child to be eligible for special education services in the area of Emotional or Behavior Disorders states that the category **may include**, but are not limited to the medically diagnosed disorders listed and described below.

a. Schizophrenia

A psychosis or impairment of thinking in which the interpretation of reality and of daily events is severely abnormal. Signs of schizophrenia include delusions, prominent hallucinations for much of the day, incoherence, lack of or inappropriate display of emotions, and bizarre delusions (such as talking with Martians). A person may also exhibit problems or decreased ability to function in work, participate in social interactions, and exhibit appropriate personal hygiene. Schizophrenia usually appears during adolescence or early adulthood. The cause is unknown; however, many believe that it is an inherited disorder.

Treatment of Schizophrenia

Treatment of schizophrenia includes pharmacotherapy (medications) using antipsychotic medications, such as Risperdal, Risperidone, and Haldol (three of the many prescribed medications) combined with psychosocial interventions. The psychosocial interventions include supportive therapy with family, educational interventions, and vocational rehabilitation when appropriate.

b. Affective disorders

1. Depression

A major depressive disorder is not simply sadness or grief, but is a genuine psychiatric illness that affects both the mind and body. Those who are depressed tend to retreat from human relationships, have trouble functioning in society, appear to be unable to enjoy life, and may even feel suicidal. Physical symptoms may include hallowness around eyes, uninflected speech, and a slowed pace. When one is nearing depression, there will be a change in that person's physical demeanor. There is often a noticeable slowing down or "dragging," or a speeding up or agitation. Lack of response to environmental changes, fatigue or loss of energy, poor appetite, insomnia, and suicidal behavior are all warning signs of clinical depression.

Treatment of Depression

Treatment for depression involves a multifaceted approach. Psychosocial interventions, such as family and individual therapy coupled with pharmacotherapy (medication) interventions such as Wellbutrin, Imipramine, Trazodone, and Effexor (some of the many medications used to treat depression) have been found to be affective.

2. Manic-Depressive Illness: (Bi-Polar)

Bi-Polar is an alternating pattern of emotional highs and high-spirited behavior (manic) and emotional lows (depression). The manic episodes and depressive episodes may alternate rapidly every few days. The mood swings experienced by one with this illness is unlike the mood swings that all people experience. Extreme and unpredictable mood swings from highly excited euphoria to the darkest depths of despair and depression are likely to be experienced by those affected by bi-polar disorder. The elation and depression occurs without relation to the circumstances. It is common to experience two or more complete cycles (a manic episode with a major depression episode with no period of remission) within a year.

Treatment of Bi-polar

Treatment of Bi-Polar Disorder is most effective through the use of medications, such as Lithium and Neuroleptics, along with psychosocial therapy. This would include intense patient-therapist interactions as well as family therapy.

3. Seasonal Affective Disorder (SAD)

SAD is a depression caused by a specific season of the year, most often winter. Some behaviors which may be exhibited include, headaches, irritability, low energy level, and crying spells. One with SAD may tend to sleep a great deal in the winter and may gain weight. The cause is not known and usually begins in adolescents or young adults. The depression experienced by people experiencing SAD is much more significant than the gloomy, dullness felt by many people during the winter months. This disorder is one that is not taken seriously by many people.

Treatment of Seasonal Affective Disorder

Treatment of SAD can be through anti-depressant medications as well as a special designed heat and light lamp.

c. Anxiety Disorders

Anxiety is a common emotion, and is often helpful when adapting to stressful situations, however, to some, anxiety is a painful or apprehensive uneasiness about something impending or an anticipated ill fortune. Some signs and symptoms of an anxiety disorder may include rapid heartbeat or respiration, tremors, stomach pains, motor tension (trembling, inability to relax), perspiring, dry mouth, dizziness, insomnia, and possible drug abuse to avoid symptoms. Anxiety, in the field of mental health, refers to tension or terror about an unidentified danger. One important characteristic about anxiety is that the person experiencing this is not able to determine what danger they are afraid of; they can only communicate that they are fearful of something.

Treatment of Anxiety Disorders

Treatment of anxiety disorders may include medications such as Antihistamines, Benzodiazepines or Buspar, coupled with intense treatment, including both individual and family therapy.

d. Phobias

A phobia is a persistent, irrational fear of something, either an object or a situation. This phobia produces a compelling desire to avoid the feared object or situation. One who has a phobia is unable to control his or her emotions and may try to avoid the object creating the phobia at all costs. There are some students who experience school phobias, at which rate, will try to avoid school at all costs.

Treatment of Phobias

The most effective treatment of phobias includes both pharmacotherapy as well as direct psychosocial therapy. Medications that may be prescribed may include but are not limited to Buspar or Antidepressants such as Imipramine or Nortriptyline.

e. Conduct Disorders

Conduct disorders are a group of behavioral and emotional problems in children and adolescents. These children have great difficulty following rules and behaving in a socially acceptable way. They are often viewed by others as being "bad" or delinquent, rather than mentally ill. Children with conduct disorders may exhibit some of the following behaviors: aggression toward people or animals, destruction of property, deceitfulness, lying, stealing, or a serious violation of rules. Many children with conduct disorders also experience coexisting conditions such as mood disorders, anxiety, substance abuse, ADHD, or learning problems.

Treatment of conduct disorders

Treatment of children with conduct disorders can be challenging. It is essential that treatment be provided in a variety of settings. Often times the child's uncooperative attitude, fear, and distrust causes difficulty as well. Behavior therapy and psychotherapy are usually necessary to help the child appropriately express and control anger. Treatment is often very time consuming and lengthy as establishing new attitudes and behavior patterns take time.

6. Hearing Impairment (HI)

A Hearing Impairment means a diminished sensitivity to sound that is expressed in terms of standard audiological measures. A hearing impairment has the potential to affect educational, communicative, or social functioning that may result in the need for special education instruction and related services.

The causes of a hearing impairment are usually classified as to whether they are exogenous or endogenous. Exogenous causes stem from factors outside the body such as disease, toxicity, or injury. Endogenous hearing impairments are inherited from the parents' genes.

Educational approaches for Hearing Impairments

Today, more than 60% of the deaf children in the United States attend local school programs, and many are included into the regular classrooms at least part of the time. The most difficult problem in educating deaf students is teaching spoken language to children who cannot hear. Many deaf students are not able to communicate effectively with schoolmates. Some educators use a primarily oral approach to education of hearing-impaired students, emphasizing the development of speech and related skills. Other educators use a total communication approach, using sign language and fingerspelling simultaneously with speech. Early detection of hearing loss and preschool education are critical to the success that most hearing impaired students will experience in school.

7. Mild Moderate Mentally Impaired (MMMI)

Mentally Impaired (MI) refers to students with significantly subaverage general intellectual functioning resulting in or associated with concurrent deficits in adaptive behavior that may require special education instruction and related services. A student's intellectual functioning, as indicated by an intelligence quotient (IQ) must be below 70 in order to be considered in the range of mild-moderate mentally impaired. A student must also indicate a delay in adaptive functioning which is related to the student's personal independence and social responsibility

Students with mild to moderate mental impairments make up 80 to 85% of the people identified as mentally impaired. In the majority of these cases, the cause is unknown. Although there is no direct proof that social and familial interactions cause mental impairments, it is generally believed that these influences cause most mild cases of mental impairments.

Educational approaches for mild-moderate mental impairments
The trends of educating students with mild mental impairments is changing. Traditionally, the students with MMMI were educated in a self-contained classroom with other students with MMMI. However, today, increasing numbers of students with MMMI are spending all or part of their school day in a regular classroom with supplemental instruction provided by a resource teacher. Simply putting a child in a regular education classroom does not mean that the child will be immediately successful. Systematically planning for the student's integration into the classroom through team activities and group investigation projects and directly training all students in specific skills for interaction with one another are just some of the methods for increasing the chances of these students to be successful in a regular class placement. Peer tutoring has also proven to be very effective.

Many children with mild mental impairments are educated in the regular classrooms with extra help provided as needed. They can generally master standard academic skills. In school, students with moderate mental impairments are usually taught communication, self-help, daily living, and vocational skills along with limited academics.

8. Moderate Severe Mentally Impaired (MSMI)

Moderate-Severe Mentally Impaired refers to students with significantly subaverage general intellectual functioning resulting in or associated with concurrent deficits in adaptive behavior that may require special education instruction and related services. A student's intellectual functioning as indicated by an intelligence quotient (IQ) must be below 50 to be considered moderate-severely mentally impaired. A student must also indicate a delay in his or her ability to be independent and socially responsible, which is considered a student's adaptive functioning.

Educational approaches for moderate to severe mental impairments

The self-contained special education classroom is a common educational placement for students with moderate to severe mental impairments. Developing functional curriculum goals for students with moderate to severe mental impairments is the goal for most educators.

Curriculum choices for students with MMMI include developing goals around the domains that represent the person as he or she lives, work, plays, and moves through the community. Personal maintenance and development, homemaking and community life, vocation, leisure, and travel are the five domains that many curriculums for mentally impaired students are based.

One effective technique to use with students with moderate to severe mental impairments is task analysis. This is a method in which large skills are broken down and sequenced into a series of subskills. A teacher breaks the task into small, easier to succeed subtasks. These subtasks are sequenced in the natural order in which they should be performed. In spite of their severe mental impairment, these students **can learn**. Their curricula stresses function, communication, and self help skills.

If students are given repeated opportunities to respond and practice as well as positive reinforcement for appropriate behavior, they are much more likely to be successful.

9. Other Health Impaired (OHI)

Other Health Impaired (OHI) includes a broad range of medically diagnosed chronic or acute health conditions that may adversely effect academic functioning and result in the need for special education instruction and related services. The decision that a specific health condition qualifies under the Other Health Impaired criteria will be determined by the impact of the condition on academic functioning rather than by the diagnostic or medical label given the condition.

Criteria to be deemed eligible for special education services in the area of OHI states that there must be a medically diagnosed chronic or acute health condition that affects academic functioning. Examples of these medically diagnosed chronic or acute health conditions include but are not limited to the examples listed below.

a. ADD/ADHD

Attention **D**eficit **D**isorder describes a child who *is not* hyperactive, but ADD can be very difficult and problematic for a child. Children with ADD are generally not disruptive in the classroom and their behaviors are usually not annoying or noticeable to the teacher. ADD can cause a child to underachieve in the classroom and experience low self-esteem. Some behavioral characteristics of a child with ADD may include being easily distracted by extraneous stimuli, difficulty listening and following directions, difficulty focusing and sustaining attention, difficulty concentrating and attending to task, inconsistent performance on school work, disorganized (can't find paper, pencils, books), poor study skills, and struggles to work independently.

Attention **D**eficit **D**isorder with **H**yperactivity describes a child who has the components as mentioned above in addition to a hyperactivity component. Along with all the characteristics described above, the child with the hyperactivity component will also exhibit a high activity level (always in constant motion, fidgets with hands or feet, falls from chair), impulsivity, lack of self-control (blurts out, can't wait for turn, interrupts, talks excessively), difficulty with transitions/changing activities, aggressive behavior, social immaturity, low self-esteem, and high frustration.

Educational and medical approaches for ADD/ADHD

Treatment of ADD/ADHD must include a multifaceted approach. It may include behavior modification at home and school, counseling, cognitive therapy (stop and think techniques), social skills training, providing a physical outlet, parent education and pharmacotherapy or medications. There are many medications found useful in treating ADD/ADHD, those medications include, but are not limited to Stimulants such as Ritalin, (methylphenidate, generic of Ritalin), Dexedrine, Adderall and Tofranil (imipramine, generic of Tofranil).

b. Chronic Fatigue Syndrome

Someone with chronic fatigue syndrome may suffer from persistent or relapsing fatigue that lasts 6 or more consecutive months. All other known diseases, infections, or psychiatric illnesses that might cause these symptoms must be ruled out. A person with Chronic Fatigue Syndrome must have four or more of the following criteria which can not be explained for any other reason. 1) sore throat, 2) painful lymph nodes in the neck or armpits, 3) prolonged fatigue following previously tolerated exercise, 4) new generalized headaches, 5) unexplained muscle soreness, 6) pain that moves from one joint to another without evidence of redness or swelling, 7) impaired memory and concentration, and 8) sleep disturbance.

Treatment of Chronic Fatigue Syndrome

Chronic Fatigue Syndrome is a syndrome of symptoms and in most cases there is no serious underlying disease causing it. There is no real "treatment" for this syndrome. In most cases, doctors will treat the symptoms that develop due to the syndrome itself.

c. Cystic Fibrosis

Cystic Fibrosis is an inherited disease that affects both the respiratory and the digestive systems. It is the most common fatal hereditary disease in white children. It occurs in boys and girls equally and is inherited on a recessive basis, which means that a child can have Cystic Fibrosis if both parents are carriers of the disease. Cystic Fibrosis affects the mucus and sweat glands of the body. As a child gets older, chronic respiratory disease may develop, including bronchitis, a collapsed lung due to blockage of airways, pneumonia, or fibrosis of the lung. Cystic Fibrosis is very serious and ultimately fatal.

Treatment of Cystic Fibrosis

Treatment of cystic fibrosis is a long-term process, and frequent checkups are important. The child should be given a pancreatic enzyme to supply the missing digestive enzymes. There are also special exercises that parents can perform to loosen and promote drainage of the mucus. This involves tapping or pounding on the child's back several times each day, to assist in loosening the mucus. Many children and young adults with this condition are able to lead active lives. With continued research and treatment techniques, the long-range outlook for children affected by Cystic Fibrosis is improving.

d. Epilepsy

Epilepsy is a seizure disorder that briefly interrupts the normal electrical activity of the brain to cause seizures. Seizures are characterized by a variety of symptoms including uncontrolled movements of the body, disorientation or confusion, or loss of consciousness. Epilepsy may result from a head injury, stroke, brain tumor, lead poisoning, genetic conditions, or severe infections like meningitis or encephalitis. In over 70 percent of cases, no cause for epilepsy is identified.

Seizures Epileptic seizures vary in intensity and symptoms depending on what part of the brain is involved. Seizures are classified as simple partial, complex partial, absence seizures, and grand mal seizures (convulsions).

Simple partial seizures cause people to experience uncontrollable jerky motions of a body part, sight or hearing impairment, sudden sweating, nausea, and feelings of fear.

Complex partial seizures last for only one or two minutes. The person experiencing the seizure may appear to be in a trance and may move randomly with no control over body movements. This form of a seizure may be preceded by an *"aura"* or a warning sensation.

Absence seizures are characterized by a sudden, momentary loss or impairment of consciousness. Overt symptoms are often an upward staring of the eyes, a staggering gait, or a twitching of facial muscles. No aura occurs prior to the seizure. Following the seizure, the person resumes activity without realizing that the seizure has occurred.

Grand mal seizures involve the whole brain. This type of seizure is often signaled by an involuntary scream, caused by contraction of the muscles that control breathing. As loss of consciousness sets in, the entire body is gripped by a jerking muscular contraction. The face reddens, breathing stops, and the back arches. Subsequently, alternate contractions and relaxation of the muscles throw the body into sometimes violent agitation such that the person may be subject to serious injury. After the convulsion subsides, the person is exhausted and may sleep heavily. Confusion, nausea, and sore muscles are often experienced upon awakening, and the person may have no memory of the seizure. Attacks occur at varying intervals - in some people as seldom as once a year and in others as frequent as several times a day.

Medical and Educational approaches for Epilepsy
There is no cure for epilepsy, but symptoms of the disorder may be treated. The majority of children with epilepsy can be helped with anticonvulsant medications such as Tegretol, Depakene, Depakote or Klonopin. Medications can sharply reduce and even eliminate seizures in many cases. All children with epilepsy will benefit from a realistic understanding of their condition and from accepting and supportive attitudes on the part of teachers and classmates.

e. Diabetes
Diabetes is a disorder of metabolism that affects the way the body absorbs and breaks down sugars and starches in food. It is a common childhood disease and affects about 1 in 600 school-aged children. A child with diabetes will lack energy and many important parts of the body, such as the eyes and kidneys, can be affected by untreated diabetes. Early symptoms of diabetes include thirst, headaches, loss of weight, frequent urination, and cuts that are slow to heal.

Medical and Educational approaches for Diabetes

Children with diabetes have insufficient insulin, which is a hormone normally produced in the body. To regulate this condition, insulin must be injected into the body daily. A specific and regular diet as well as a regular exercise program are usually suggested also.

Teachers should be aware of the symptoms of insulin reaction, also called *diabetic shock*. It can result from taking too much insulin, from strenuous exercise, or from a missed or delayed meal. Symptoms of insulin reaction or diabetic shock include faintness, dizziness, blurred vision, drowsiness, and nausea. A child may appear irritable or have a marked personality change. In most case, giving a child some form of concentrated sugar (sugar cube, a glass of fruit juice, or a candy bar) should end the reaction within a few minutes.

f. Hemophilia

Hemophilia is a blood disease that does not allow the blood to clot. It is caused by genes that are recessive and sex-linked (carried on the sex chromosome) so the disorder almost always occurs in boys, not girls. The major problem for people with hemophilia is not the superficial external cuts, but the uncontrolled internal bleeding. Signs and symptoms of Hemophilia include large or deep bruises, pain and swelling of joints, blood in the urine, and prolonged bleeding from cuts or injuries.

Medical and Educational approaches for Hemophilia

Most people with hemophilia can live a relatively normal life. Exercise, medication, and in some instances surgery may be necessary to treat hemophilia. In school, a student may need to be excused from some physical activities and may need the use of a wheelchair during times where the student is experiencing difficulties.

g. Asthma

Asthma is characterized by episodes of narrowing of the bronchial tubes in the lungs. Normally, these tubes narrow only as protective reaction to prevent harmful substances from entering the lungs. With Asthma, the bronchial tubes narrow too much, too often, and too easily in response to a variety of substances that ordinarily would not damage the lungs. Signs and symptoms of Asthma include shortness of breath, coughing, tightness of the chest, and wheezing.

Medical and Educational approaches for Asthma

Asthma is one of the most frequently cited reasons for missing school. Chronic absenteeism makes it difficult for the child with Asthma to maintain performance at grade level. The majority of children with Asthma who receive medical and psychological support, successfully complete school and lead normal lives. Treatment of Asthma is most often done through medication dispersed using inhalers and nebulizers. An inhaler can be used periodically throughout the day when an asthmatic senses an attack or a need to clear the airway passages. A nebulizer is used for more severe instances of an asthma attack. Once children have been informed and are educated about their condition, they are often able to "feel" when they need to use their inhaler to proactively prevent an asthmatic attack from developing. These children need to be allowed to use their inhaler when they feel it is necessary.

10. Physically Impaired

A Physical Impairment is a medically diagnosed chronic physical impairment, either congenital or acquired, that may adversely affect physical or academic functioning and result in the need for special education and related services.

Criteria to be deemed eligible for special education services in the area of Physically Impaired states that there must be a medically diagnosed chronic physical impairment that affects academic functioning. Examples of these medically diagnosed chronic physical impairments may include but are not limited to the examples listed below.

a. Burns

Burns are the leading type of injury in childhood. Most often, burns result from household accidents but sometimes they are caused by child abuse. Serious burns can cause complications in other organs, long-term physical limitations, and psychological difficulties. Children with serious burn injuries usually experience pain, scarring, limitations of motion, lengthy hospitalizations, and repeated surgeries.

Educational information about burns

The disfigurement caused by severe burns can affect a child's behavior and self-image, especially if teachers and peers react negatively. When a child is returning to class after a prolonged absence resulting from an extensive burn injury, it may be advisable for the teacher, parents, or other involved persons to explain to classmates the nature of the child's injury and appearance.

b. Limb Deficiency

A limb deficiency is the absence or partial loss of an arm or leg. A congenital limb deficiency or absence of a limb at birth is rare. Acquired limb deficiencies (amputations) are more common and are often the result of surgery or an accident.

Educational information about limb deficiencies

Some students may use a prosthesis or an artificial limb to assist with a variety of tasks and to create a more normal appearance. Some students, however, prefer not to use a prosthesis. Most children become quite proficient at using their remaining limbs. Some children who are missing both arms, for example may need to re-learn different tasks and skills, such as to write with their feet. Unless children have other impairments in addition to the absence of limbs, they should be able to function in a regular classroom with only minor modifications.

11. Severely Multiply Impaired

Severely Multiply Impaired involves severe learning and developmental problems resulting from two or more disability conditions determined by assessment.

A student is deemed eligible as being severely multiply impaired if the student meets the entrance criteria for two or more of the following disabilities:

1. **Hearing Impaired**
2. **Physically Impaired**
3. **Moderate-Severe Mentally Impaired**
4. **Visually Impaired**
5. **Emotional or Behavior disorders**
6. **Autism**

12. Specific Learning Disabilities (SLD)

A Specific Learning Disability is defined as a condition within the individual affecting learning relative to potential.

1. A specific learning disability is manifested by interference with acquisition, organization, storage, retrieval, manipulation, or expression of information inhibiting the individual to learn at an adequate rate when provided with the usual developmental opportunities and instruction from a regular school environment.

2. A specific learning disability is demonstrated by a significant discrepancy between a student's general intellectual ability and academic achievement in one of more of the following areas: oral expression, listening comprehension, mathematical calculation, mathematical reasoning, basic reading skills, reading comprehension, or written expression.

3. A specific learning disability is demonstrated primarily in academic functioning, but may also affect self-esteem, career development, and life adjustment skills. A specific learning disability may occur with, but cannot be primarily the result of a visual, hearing, motor, or mental impairment; an emotional disorder; environmental, cultural, or economic influences, or a history of an inconsistent education program.

Educational approaches for Learning Disabilities

There are two basic approaches to educating learning disabled children: ability training and skills training. Ability training includes instructional activities designed to remediate a child's weakness in underlying basic abilities.

Skill training is based on the belief that a child's performance deficit is the problem, not a sign of an underlying disability. In skill training, remediation is based on direct instruction of precisely defined skills, many opportunities for practice and repetition, and a direct measurement of a child's progress. Research has shown this approach to be effective.

Children with learning disabilities are educated in a variety of placements and receive many different delivery arrangements, but most students with learning disabilities are educated in the regular classroom for the majority of the school day. A consultant teacher may help the regular classroom teacher work with children with learning disabilities in the classroom providing support and modifications of regular classroom assignments. The resource room may also be used to deliver service to children with learning disabilities. This would involve a specially trained teacher to work with the child on a particular skill deficit for one or more periods a day in a classroom away from the regular education classroom.

13. Speech or Language Impairment

This disability area is divided into 4 categories of Speech or Language Impairments. Those 4 categories are: a) Fluency Disorder, b) Voice Disorder, c) Articulation Disorder and d) Language Disorder.

a. Fluency Disorder

A fluency disorder is the intrusion of repetition of sounds, syllables, and words; prolongation of sounds; avoidance of words; silent blocks; or inappropriate inhalation, exhalation, or phonation patterns. These patterns may also be accompanied by facial and body movements associated with the effort to speak. Fluency patterns that can be attributed only to dialectical, cultural, or ethnic differences or to the influence of a foreign language should not be identified as a disorder.

b. Voice Disorder

A voice disorder is the absence of voice or presence of abnormal quality, pitch, resonance, loudness, or duration in ones voice. Voice patterns that can be attributed only to dialectical, cultural, or ethnic differences, or to the influence of a foreign language should not be identified as a disorder.

c. Articulation Disorder

An articulation disorder is the absence of or incorrect production of speech sounds that are developmentally appropriate. Articulation patterns that can be attributed only to dialectical, cultural, or ethnic differences or to the influence of a foreign language should not be identified as a disorder.

d. Language Disorder

A language disorder is a breakdown in communication as characterized by problems in expressing needs, ideas, or information that may be accompanied by problems in understanding. Language patterns that can be attributed only to dialectical, cultural, or ethnic differences or to the influence of a foreign language should not be identified as a disorder.

As many as 5% of all school-age children have speech impairments serious enough to require speech assistance. Nearly twice as many boys as girls have speech impairments and children with articulation problems represent the largest category of speech/language impairments. Although some speech disorders do have an organic cause, most disorders cannot be attributed to a physical condition. The most common fluency disorder is stuttering.

Educational approaches for Speech and Language Impairments

Different types of communication disorders require different approaches to remediation. This is usually done in one on one or group settings with a specially trained speech and language pathologist. Most of these children with speech disorders do attend regular education classes and then receive the speech therapy throughout the school day for short periods of time. The specific activities worked on in the speech sessions should then be generalized and used in the regular education settings as much as possible.

14. Traumatic Brain Injury (TBI)

Traumatic Brain Injury is an acquired injury to the brain caused by an external physical force, resulting in total or partial functional disability or psychosocial impairment, or both, that may adversely affect a child's educational performance and result in the need for special education and related services. The term applies to open or closed head injuries resulting in impairments in one or more of the following areas: cognition, speech/language, memory, attention, reasoning, abstract thinking, judgment, problem-solving, sensory, perceptual and motor abilities, psychosocial behavior, physical functions, and information processing. The term **does not apply** to brain injuries that are congenital or degenerative, or brain injuries induced by birth trauma.

Most traumatic brain injuries are caused by automobile, motorcycle, and bicycle accidents; falls, assaults, gunshot wounds, and child abuse. Many children who have suffered serious head injury also experience subsequent problems in learning, behavior, and adjustment. The children may also display inappropriate or exaggerated behavior ranging from extreme aggressiveness to apathetic behavior. Children may also have difficulty paying attention and retaining new information.

Educational approaches for Traumatic Brain Injuries
Children who re-enter school will experience deficits from their injuries compounded by an extended absence from school. These students will likely require academic, psychological, and family support. Few educational programs have been specifically designed for this population, however, these children will most likely need special services in order to successfully progress in their learning.

15. Visually Impaired

The term visually impaired means a medically verified visual impairment accompanied by a limitation in sight that interferes with acquiring information or interaction with the environment to the extent that special education and related services may be needed.

Criteria that must be met to be deemed eligible for special education services in the area of visually impaired states that there must be a medically verified visual impairment accompanied by limitation in sight. Examples of these medically diagnosed visual impairments may include but are not limited to the examples listed below.

a. Cataract

A cataract is a clouding of the eye lens. Its cause could be hereditary, due to an infection, severe malnutrition, drugs during pregnancy, or from trauma. Symptoms include a whitish appearance of the pupil and blurred vision.

Medical treatment for Cataracts

The only medical treatment for cataracts is surgery. Cataracts should be removed within the first few months of life if acuity is to develop normally. Contact lenses or glasses may help with vision acuity. A child with a central, unoperated cataract may have some unusual head positions, since the child is essentially "looking around" the cataract to help vision. Magnification is helpful in some cases.

b. Glaucoma

Glaucoma is the leading cause of blindness. If detected and treated early, glaucoma need not cause blindness or even severe vision loss. Glaucoma is a group of diseases of the eye which causes progressive damage to the optic nerve due to increased pressure within the eyeball. As the optic nerve deteriorates, blind spots develop. If left untreated, the result may be total blindness. Signs and symptoms of glaucoma include blurred vision (usually in one eye), halos appearing around lights, pain in the eye, and a reddening of the eye.

Medical treatment for Glaucoma

Glaucoma is often treated through surgery. An operation is performed which is used to create a drainage hole in the iris. This is done by a laser and is very quick with few repercussions.

c. Retinitis Pigmentosa (R.P.)

R.P. is when the retina in both eyes slowly deteriorate. There is often no apparent reason for its occurrence. As the disease progresses, night vision deteriorates and peripheral vision is lost producing "tunnel vision" This often leads to legal blindness.

Medical treatment for R.P

There is no known treatment for R.P. A variety of optical aids may be effective, such as magnifiers, telescopes, and prism lenses.

d. Albanism

This is an inherited deficiency of the pigmentation in the eye. It may involve the entire body or just part of the body. Impaired vision, due to Albanism, usually ranges between 20/70 and 20/200.

Medical Treatment for Albanism

Treatment of albanism is most often with the use of tinted or pinhole contact lenses, absorptive lenses, or optical aids, although these may not always be helpful. Adjusting the lighting and conditions for individuals or wearing sunglasses and seeking shade when outdoors, is essential for one who is very sensitive to bright lighting.

e. Nystagmus

Nystagmus is an involuntary, rhythmical, repeated movement of one or both eyes in any or all fields of gaze. Movements may be horizontal, vertical, or circular and are often rapid and jerky. Nystagmus may accompany neurological disorders or may be caused from a reaction to certain drugs.

Medical treatment for Nystagmus

There is no know treatment for Nystagmus; however, certain types of jerky nystagmus show improvement in childhood. Children with nystagmus may tend to lose their place in beginning reading instruction and may need help through the use of an underline (a card to underline the sentence that they are reading), or a typoscope (a card with a hole to view one word or line at a time). As children with nystagmus mature, they seem to need these support devices less often, as they tend to compensate in other ways.

Educational Approaches for Visual Impairments

Teachers of visually impaired children need specialized skills along with knowledge and creativity. Most children who are blind learn to read using Braille. They may also learn to type and use special equipment for mathematics, social studies and science, as well as learn, feel and read regular print while listening to it on a taped recording. Children with low vision should learn to use their residual vision as efficiently as possible. They may use optical aids and large print to read regular type. Encourage all visually impaired children to develop and utilize their listening skills.

Section II

The
Special Education
Process

The Special Education Process

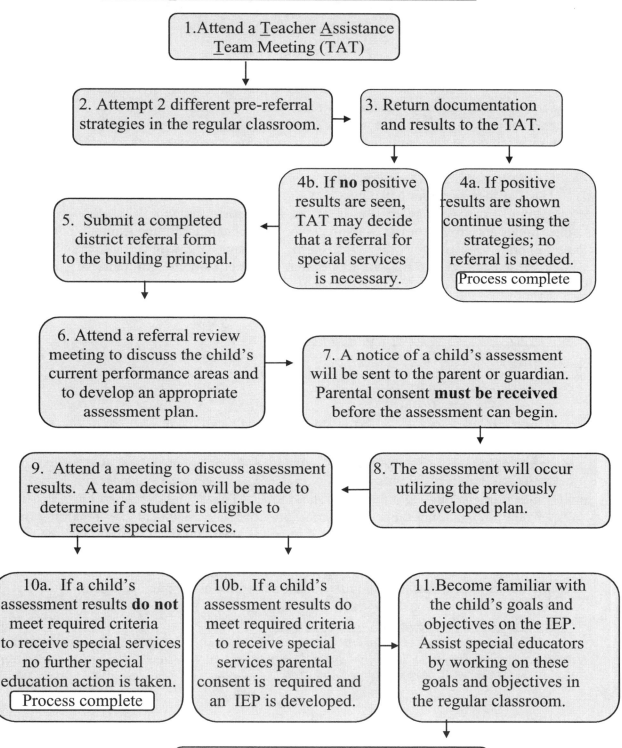

1. Attend a <u>T</u>eacher <u>A</u>ssistance <u>T</u>eam Meeting (TAT)

2. Attempt 2 different pre-referral strategies in the regular classroom.

3. Return documentation and results to the TAT.

4b. If **no** positive results are seen, TAT may decide that a referral for special services is necessary.

4a. If positive results are shown continue using the strategies; no referral is needed.
Process complete

5. Submit a completed district referral form to the building principal.

6. Attend a referral review meeting to discuss the child's current performance areas and to develop an appropriate assessment plan.

7. A notice of a child's assessment will be sent to the parent or guardian. Parental consent **must be received** before the assessment can begin.

8. The assessment will occur utilizing the previously developed plan.

9. Attend a meeting to discuss assessment results. A team decision will be made to determine if a student is eligible to receive special services.

10a. If a child's assessment results **do not** meet required criteria to receive special services no further special education action is taken.
Process complete

10b. If a child's assessment results do meet required criteria to receive special services parental consent is required and an IEP is developed.

11. Become familiar with the child's goals and objectives on the IEP. Assist special educators by working on these goals and objectives in the regular classroom.

12. Attend at least one periodic and one annual review for each student with an IEP.

Special Education Process

1. Attend a Teacher Assistance Team (TAT) meeting

TAT is a committee formed to assist regular education teachers who have a student who is struggling to learn or whose behavior is interfering with his or her own or other's ability to learn in the regular education classroom. Inform a member of the TAT committee that you are interested in coming to the meeting prior to the next meeting date. Your name will be put on the agenda to ensure that the concerns regarding your student will be discussed that day. Be prepared to share information with the team regarding this student's academic and/or behavioral difficulties, things that you have already tried in the classroom, progress or regression that you have seen throughout the school year, and other important information that you feel would be beneficial for the team to know. After discussion, the team will offer suggestions, providing you with a number of different intervention strategies to try with this student in the classroom. An intervention strategy is a planned, systematic effort by the regular education staff to resolve apparent learning or behavioral problems within the regular education classroom.

Note to teachers about parent(s) or guardian(s)

It is important to keep parents or guardians informed of what is happening at school. If you haven't already talked to this student's parent(s) or guardian(s) regarding the concerning issues at school, do so now.

2. Return to the classroom and try at least 2 of the suggested strategies.

Special education law requires that before a student can be referred for a special education assessment, the district must conduct and document at least two instructional strategies, alternatives, or interventions attempted to assist the student with his or her difficulties in the regular education classroom. The student's classroom teacher is responsible for initiating the strategies and providing the documentation regarding these intervention strategies. It is encouraged that approximately 30 days, if possible, be given to try the different interventions, in order to give the interventions a chance to work.

The law does state that the special education assessment team may waive this requirement if they determine that the student's need for assessment is urgent.

Note to teachers about parent(s) or guardian(s)

Inform this student's parent(s) or guardian(s) that you did discuss their child's challenging behaviors or learning difficulties at the TAT meeting. Also tell them about the different intervention strategies you will be trying in the classroom.

3. After approximately 30 days, present your documentation and results of the interventions to the TAT team.

Bring your documentation with you to the meeting for the TAT members to review and discuss the results. Important information to bring to the meeting would include **what** intervention(s) you've tried, **how** the intervention(s) have worked, **if** one intervention worked better than another, or any other information you feel would be beneficial for the team to know.

Note to teachers about parent(s) or guardian(s)

Before returning to the TAT meeting, it is important to inform this child's parent(s) or guardian(s) of the results that occurred while implementing the intervention strategies in the regular education classroom.

4a. If positive results are shown with the use of these intervention strategies, continue to utilize the strategies within the classroom.

The team would likely not see that a referral for special education services is necessary.

Note to teachers about parent(s) or guardian(s)

Inform this child's parent(s) or guardian(s) that the intervention strategies did seem to produce positive results and that you will be continuing to use those strategies with the child in the regular education classroom.

4b. If no positive results are seen, and perhaps even worsening results are noted, the TAT members will probably decide that a referral for special education services is necessary.

Note to teachers about parent(s) or guardian(s):

Inform the child's parent(s) or guardian(s) that the intervention strategies attempted did not provide positive results and therefore, the TAT believes that a referral for special education services would be beneficial for the student. Explain to the parent that a "referral" means a formal and ongoing process to review information related to a student who is showing potential signs of needing special education and related services. An effective referral process will need to utilize relevant information from a full range of sources including home, school, and community. Emphasize to the parents that their involvement in this process is essential.

5. Complete the district "Referral for Special Education" form.

You will need to complete the form, providing the information that you documented regarding the pre-referral intervention strategies that were tried and the results that occurred. You will also need to provide student-specific demographic information regarding name, age, grade, parent's name, etc. Once you have completed the form as thoroughly as possible, you will need to sign the form and then submit it to the building principal for his or her signature as well.

Note to teachers about parent(s) or guardian(s)

Inform the parent(s) or guardian(s) that you have completed and submitted the district referral form to the building principal, and that a meeting will soon be held to discuss the referral. Parent(s) or guardian(s) have the right to be informed in advance of the date and time of this meeting. Encourage the parent(s) or guardian(s) to make every effort to attend this first meeting, as their input will be critical.

6. Attend a referral review meeting.

After the principal has signed the district referral form, the school psychologist and special education staff will be informed of the referral. A special education staff member will be responsible for arranging the referral review meeting. At the meeting, a special education team will be formed. The team will discuss the issues and concerns surrounding this student and will develop an assessment plan to be followed during the referral process.

A student's team will consist of the student's parent(s) or guardian(s), regular education classroom teacher, school psychologist, principal, and one or more of the special education staff who will be involved in the special education assessment. Different special education staff will be involved depending on the needs of the students. If academic concerns are the issue, a Learning Disabled special education teacher will be involved; if behaviors are the issue, the Emotional/Behavioral Disorders teacher would be involved; if Speech is an issue, the Speech and Language teacher would be involved. If there is a combination of issues, perhaps two or more specialized special education teachers would be involved.

At the meeting, a referral review will be completed as well as an assessment plan. The following information will be utilized in order to complete the documents described above.

A - Referral Review Form

Student's present level of performance: The team will discuss and review the student's performance in the following areas.

1. **Intellectual functioning:** This refers to a student's cognitive ability or IQ.
2. **Academic performance:** This is how well the student is achieving the grade-level academic requirements in the regular education classroom. Specific information about a child who is struggling to find success in the grade-level curriculums will be addressed. The regular classroom teacher will be asked to provide information regarding the student's academic performance in the classroom.
3. **Communicative status:** This area examines how the student is able to communicate with others (age-peers, older peers, adults, teachers) in order to get his or her needs met. Parent(s) or guardian(s) and classroom teachers will be asked to provide information in this area.
4. **Motor ability:** Discussion in this area will include both fine and gross motor skills. Activities such as handwriting and cutting with scissors may be discussed for fine motor skills, and outdoor or physical ed. activities such as

running, jumping rope, and skipping may be discussed for gross motor skills. Parent(s) or guardian(s) and classroom teachers would be asked to provide information in this area.

5. **Vocational Potential:** This area must only be addressed for students who will be 14 years of age or older or entering 9th grade during the effective dates of the IEP. The 5 areas of transition will be considered. These areas are 1) jobs and job training, 2) recreation and leisure, 3) home-independent living, 4) community participation and 5) post-secondary training and learning opportunities. The area of vocational potential will rarely be utilized for elementary students.

6. **Sensory Status:** This area includes both visual and hearing components. Any concerns regarding a student's sight or hearing abilities will be discussed. Information gathered from the student's parent(s) or guardian(s) will be essential.

7. **Physical Status:** A student's overall condition of his or her health will be discussed here. Any concerns regarding the student's health in general will be addressed in this section. Parental or guardian input will be critical for this area.

8. **Emotional and Social Development:** How well a child is able to interact with peers and others in social situations as well as how a child is able to emotionally handle different situations and feelings will be discussed in this section.

9. **Behavior:** A child's behavior will be discussed here. If there are any behavioral concerns in the classroom, in the community, or at home, they will be addressed in this section. Input from teacher(s) and parent(s) or guardian(s) is important for this section.

10. **Functional Skills:** A student's functional skills, meaning how the student is able to care for him or herself and how able the student is to perform daily living skills on his or her own will be addressed in this section. Issues such as toilet training, dressing self, and feeding self will be discussed. Other functional skills will include caring for pets, keeping his or her room clean, bathing and showering self, etc. Parental or guardian input will be imperative.

Note to teachers about parent(s) or guardian(s)

It is essential that the student's parent(s) or guardian(s) be involved in this initial referral review meeting. Crucial information regarding the student's communicative status, physical status, emotional and social development, and behavior and functional skills can be provided only by the student's parent(s) or guardian(s).

B - Development of the Assessment Plan

After the referral review is completed and all of the above areas have been discussed, an assessment plan will be developed. An assessment is an evaluation of a student's strengths and weaknesses by using different testing instruments. It is important for the team to use a variety of assessment tools, both formal and informal, to gather relevant, functional, and developmental information about a student. This information can be gathered in a variety of ways.

1. **Traditional assessments** are formal, standardized tools designed to test a specific area or a student's level of functioning. They are used to gather in-depth information relating to a student's capabilities and performance. The results gathered by using formal assessments are used to compare this student to that of the performance of other students his or her age or grade-level. These tests provide information that will help to determine if your student is performing well above, well below, or equal to other student's his or her age or grade-level. (See examples and descriptions of common traditional assessments on pages 44-56).

2. **Nontraditional assessments** are other ways to gather valuable information. These assessments are informal methods of gathering systematic information about a student's functioning in a particular setting. These could include looking at classwork samples, observations in multiple settings, or any other helpful way to receive information and get to know the child. (See other examples of nontraditional assessment on page 57).

C - Special Education Staff Responsibility

After the team determines which assessments will be utilized, then the team must decide who is going to be responsible for administering those traditional and nontraditional assessments.

D - Completion of the "Notice of Education Assessment/Reassessment" form

All information discussed at this meeting, including the assessment methods used and the special education staff responsibility will be documented on the "Notice of Education Assessment/Reassessment" form.

7. Obtain parental consent prior to beginning to assess

A copy of the "Notice of Educational Assessment/Reassessment" will be provided to the parent(s) or guardian(s) of the student. The parent or guardian must give the final consent for the student to undergo assessments before any assessments can take place. The school **cannot** proceed with any assessment activities without the prior written consent of the student's parent or guardian.

Note to teachers about parent(s) or guardian(s)

*Inform the parent(s) or guardian(s) that they must give consent, by completing page 3 of the Notice of Educational Assessment/Reassessment form. The assessment can not begin until that form is completed. Giving consent to assess **does not mean** that the parent or guardian is giving consent for the child to __receive__ special education services. It only means that the Special Education team is given permission to test the child.*

8. Complete the Assessment

Once the permission is given by the parent(s) or guardian(s), the assessment will begin. The team must conduct the assessment within a reasonable amount of time, not to exceed 30 days from the date that the school received the parental permission to conduct the assessment. Once all assessments are complete, an Assessment Summary Report must be written. The special education team will write a report that integrates the findings from all formal and informal assessments completed. The report should include the results and interpretations of the assessments, the student's present level of performance in the areas assessed, and the team's judgments regarding eligibility for services. The assessment summary report must also have all team members' names, titles, and the date the report was written.

Note to teachers about parent(s) or guardian(s)

Inform the parent(s) or guardian(s) that once the assessment is complete a meeting will be set up in which all team members will get together to discuss the results of the assessments, and further action, if any, that the educational team is proposing. Parent(s) or guardian(s) should be given prior written notice so that they will have adequate time to make arrangements to attend the meeting.

9. Attend a meeting to discuss the assessment results

During this meeting, each team member who took part in any of the assessments will describe what assessment was utilized and the results of the assessment. *If at any time, you do not understand something that is being said, be sure and mention it; it's likely that you are not the only one with that question.* At this time, the team will provide information regarding whether this student does meet the criteria required by the state to be deemed eligible to receive special services through any of the 15 categories. (The 15 categories were described in Section I). If a child is found eligible to receive special services through a specific category, it means that through the test results, he or she has indicated that the criteria required in order to be determined eligible has been met and that justification of this has been made in the assessment summary report.

10a.- If the child does not qualify for special services, the process is complete.

If the assessment results indicate that a child **does not** qualify to receive special educational services under any one of the 15 categories, than the special education process is complete. No further special education action can be taken.

10b.- If the child does qualify for special services, further action is taken.

If the assessment results do indicate that the child does qualify for special education services an Individualized Education Plan (IEP) must be written. This can take place on the same day as the meeting to discuss the assessment results, or another meeting can be scheduled to write the IEP. If another meeting is scheduled, state law requires it to be held within 30 calendar days of the determination that the student needs special services, and it needs to be at a time when the student's parent(s) or guardian(s) can attend. Most often, it is easiest just to write the IEP on that same day as the assessment summary meeting, because it can be difficult finding dates and times where all team members are available to attend another meeting. The IEP must be written at the meeting, as it is not permissible for an IEP to be completed before the IEP meeting begins.

When writing an IEP, all team members must be present. Required team members include **1) parents, 2) special education teacher, 3) regular classroom teacher, 4)representative of the school district (a special education administrator, or school administrator) 5) other members at the parent or district discretion.**

Notes to teachers about parent(s) of guardian(s)

Encourage parent(s) or guardian(s) to ask any questions that they may have. You want to be sure that they understand everything that was discussed and decided upon so that they feel comfortable with the plan that was set up for their child.

Explanation of the Individualized Education Plan (IEP)

Purpose of the IEP:

An individualized education plan, or IEP, is the result of a process to ensure that individuals with disabilities have appropriate educational planning to accommodate their unique instructional needs, and that these needs are met in an appropriate learning environment. An IEP is a written statement for a specific student with a disability that is developed, reviewed, and revised when needed.

Writing the IEP:

The IEP must include certain components to ensure that all areas of the student's education are being met. The first component of the IEP is to make a statement which describes the student's present levels of educational performance in the following areas:

Component A:
1) intellectual functioning
2) academic performance
3) communicative status
4) motor ability
5) vocational potential
6) sensory status
7) physical status
8) emotional and social development
9) behavior
10) functional skills

Component B: After discussing the student's present level of educational performance, the team must then decide upon specific, student-based instructional needs that must be addressed.

Component C: At least one annual goal must be written for each of the needs identified by the IEP team as a priority for that year. For each goal, short-term objectives must be written as well:

Goals: The annual goals in the IEP are statements that describe what a child with a disability can reasonably be expected to accomplish within a twelve month period. There should be a direct relationship between annual goals and the student's instructional needs.

Objectives: Short term objectives are measurable, intermediate steps between the present level of performance of a student and the annual goals that are established. The objectives are developed based on a logical breakdown of the major components of the annual goals, and can serve as milestones for measuring progress toward meeting the goals.

Progress reviews: The IEP team must discuss a plan for reviewing the progress of the goals and objectives. There must be at least **one periodic review,** and **one annual review** of the student's progress towards achieving the goals and objectives set for the student.

Component D: The IEP must include a statement of the specific special education and related services to be provided to the students. The IEP must list who is responsible for providing those services, how much time each week will be provided, and the date that those services will begin.

Component E: The team must write a statement of justification which states how the team ensures that the proposed plan is going to provide for the Least Restrictive Environment for the student. The statement should include opportunities to participate and progress in the general education curriculum and other school activities as well as to state any modifications and adaptations that this student may need in order to be successful.

A modification or adaptation is a way in which the regular education curriculum or classroom environment is changed for a student with special needs in order to assist a student in being more successful in the regular education classroom. Examples of specific adaptations or modifications are provided in section II.

The IEP must be written and agreed upon by all team members.

Note to teachers about parent(s) or guardian(s)

Before a student's special education services can begin for the first time, the student's parent(s) or guardian(s) must give written consent, agreeing to the IEP and the proposed plan.

11. Know the goals and objectives on the IEP.

A classroom teacher must be familiar with a student's IEP contents, especially his or her goals and objectives and modifications that must be made within the regular education classroom.

12. Attend a periodic and annual review of the IEP.

The progress that a student is making toward his or her goals and objectives on the IEP must be reviewed **at least** two times during the year. A **periodic review** must be held at least one time during the year to discuss a student's progress. The periodic review is most often held during a Parent-Teacher Conference. An **annual review** must also be held within one year of the date on the IEP. At the annual review, the IEP will be reviewed, revised, and rewritten. If the student has progressed and met some or all of the goals and objectives on the IEP, new goals and objectives will be written to address current educational performance issues. It is at the IEP annual review that the team also determines if the student continues to show a need to receive special education services.

Note to teachers about parent(s) or guardian(s)

Encourage parent(s) or guardian(s) to attend both the periodic review and annual reviews, as their input is essential. Parent(s) or guardian(s) do have the right to request an IEP meeting at any time that they feel one is necessary. For example, if the parent(s) or guardian(s) believe their child is not progressing satisfactorily or there is a problem with the current IEP, it would be appropriate for the parent to request an IEP meeting.

©Peytral Publications Inc.

A student who receives special education services must be reassessed every 3 years to ensure that the student continues to meet eligibility criteria as well as continues to require special education services to be successful in school.

Traditional, Formal Assessments

1. Intellectual Functioning

a. Wechsler Intelligence Scales for Children - Third Edition (WISC-III)

This is a standardized test that is administered individually to children ages 6 to 16 to assess general intellectual functioning. The results of this battery of tests will also provide information regarding the student's strengths and weaknesses in specific areas of ability. The test has 13 subtests, but only 10 subtests are required to be administered in order to determine IQ scores. The test is divided into two main sections. The verbal scale which consists of 5 subtests and the performance scale which also consists of 5 subtests. The verbal scale measures how well children are able to express themselves verbally and how well they are able to understand what is being said to them. The performance scale measures the nonverbal areas of being able to perceive spatial relationships; such as putting puzzles together and being able to transfer visual information quickly.

When determining results of the WISC-III, three IQ scores are given. A Verbal IQ, using information gathered from the verbal scale subtests, a Performance IQ, utilizing information gathered from the performance scale and finally a Full Scale IQ, which is based on the performance of all scales put together.

The global IQ scores are just like **Standard Scores** and can be interpreted using the Standard Score criteria. Four factor-based Index Scores are also produced by making combinations of subtests. These Index Scores are the same as **Standard Scores** as well and can be interpreted using the Standard Score criteria. Individual subtest **Scaled Scores** are also provided. (See the **Explanation of Test Scores** section on page 55 for clarification of meanings of individual scores).

b. Wechsler Preschool and Primary Scale of Intelligence-Revised (WPPSI)

This is a test administered individually to children ages 3 years to 7 years 3 months of age. The results of this battery of tests will provide information regarding the student's strengths and weaknesses in specific areas of ability. The test is divided into two main sections. The verbal scale and the performance scale. The verbal scale measures how well children are able to express themselves verbally and how well they are able to understand what is being said to them. The performance scale measures the nonverbal areas of being able to perceive spatial relationships; such as putting puzzles together and being able to transfer visual information quickly.

When determining results of the WPPSI, three IQ scores are given. A Verbal IQ, using information gathered from the Verbal Scale subtests, a Performance IQ, utilizing information gathered from the Performance Scale and finally a Full Scale IQ, which is based on the performance of all scales put together.

The global IQ scores are just like **Standard Scores** and can be interpreted using the Standard Score criteria. Individual subtest **Scaled Scores** are also provided. (See the **Explanation of Test Scores** section on page 55 for clarification of meanings of individual scores).

c. Woodcock-Johnson Psycho-Educational Battery-Revised Test of Cognitive Ability (Part 1)

The Woodcock-Johnson test has two parts. The first part measures a student's cognitive ability and the 2nd part measures the student's school performance or achievement. Part one of this test is used to determine a student's intellectual ability. This test is administered individually and usually takes less than one hour to administer the entire standard battery. The test can be used in individuals ages 2 to 90+ years old; and has scoring norms for grade K-12, and college.

There are 21 cognitive ability tests arranged into two levels. There are 7 subtests which make up the standard battery (those subtests **must be** administered), and then there are 14 supplemental subtests which may be administered if further information is needed. One, a few, or all of these tests may be administered, depending on the additional information that is needed. This battery can be a bit difficult to administer and should be administered by a school psychologist.

Many results are produced by this assessment battery. The Broad Ability Scale, summarizes the students performance on the standard battery. A Broad Ability Extended Scale is also available; it takes into account all standard battery subtests as well as seven of the supplementary subtests. Results can also be reported by subtest, cognitive factor, and by areas of scholastic aptitude. More than 35 subtest and area results are produced and each result can be expressed as an **Age-Equivalent, Grade-Equivalent, Standard Score,** and a **Percentile Rank.** (See the **Explanation of Test Scores** section on page 55 for clarification of meanings of individual scores).

The Woodcock-Johnson III, a revised addition, is scheduled to be released in the Fall of 2000.

2. Adaptive Behavior Measures

Adaptive behavior is related to both personal independence and social responsibility. Expected adaptive behavior varies with the age of the individual. Preschool children are expected to learn to walk, talk, and interact with family members. School-aged children are expected to widen their circle of acquaintances and add academic skills to their repertoire. A student's adaptive behavior is assessed when a student is suspected of being mild-moderate or moderate-severely mentally impaired, or having Autistic characteristics.

Adaptive behavior is usually not measured directly. Instead the student's parents or teachers are used as informants about the student's current nonacademic functioning. Interviews are typically used with parents and written questionnaires are used with teachers.

a. AAMR Adaptive Behavior Scale - School (2nd Ed.) (ABS-S:2)

The ABS-S:2 is an indirect measure of adaptive and maladaptive behavior. This test can be utilized for children with mental impairments who are ages 3 - 21. This test is utilized for children without mental impairments who are ages 3 - 18. Results of the ABS-S:2 can be used to identify strengths and weaknesses in adaptive behavior, determine if a student shows below average performance in this area, and can document student progress. ABS-S:2 is a questionnaire and can be completed by professionals such as teachers. If a professional is unable to make judgments regarding the student's skill levels, than the scale is used as an interview where a trained professional asks the questions and the parent or other person who knows the student well answers the questions. Part 1 of the ABS-S:2 addresses adaptive behaviors skills related to personal independence, part 2 is concerned with social behaviors. 16 domains are assessed. Those 16 domains are then separated into "Five Factors". Those Five Factors include *1) Personal Self-Sufficiency, 2) Community Self-Sufficiency, 3) Personal-Social Responsibility, 4) Social Adjustment* and *5)Personal Adjustment.*

Results of the ABS-S:2 are described using **Percentile Ranks** and **Scaled Scores** for each of the 16 domains as well as for the Five Factor scores. A Quotient or overall test score can also be explained using **Percentile Ranks** and **Standard Scores**. **Age-Equivalent Scores** can be obtained for Part One Factors (Factors 1, 2 and 3) only. (See the **Explanation of Test Scores** section on page 55 for clarification of meanings of individual scores).

b. Vineland Adaptive Behavior Scales

The Vineland Adaptive Behavior Scales contain three separate scales: two interview editions (a survey form and an expanded form), and a classroom edition. The interview editions are used by trained interviewers with parents or others who know the students well. The survey form includes fewer items than the expanded interview form and consequently requires less administration time. The Vineland can be used for children from birth to 18 years 11 months old, and with low functioning adults.

The classroom edition is a print questionnaire completed by the student's teacher. It is appropriate for ages 3 to 12 years 11 months and takes approximately 20 minutes to completed.

Both classroom and interview editions assess four adaptive behavior domains. Those domains include *1) Communication, 2)Daily Living Skills, 3) Socialization,* and *4) Motor Skills.* Administration of the Vineland interview versions are restricted to psychologists, social workers, and other professionals with a graduate degree and specific training in individual assessment and test interpretations.

Standard Scores are used to report results of the Vineland Adaptive Behavior Scales. These Standard Scores are available for each of the four adaptive behavior domains as well as for the total test or Composite score which is a summary of the four domains. (See the **Explanation of Test Scores** section on page 55 for clarification of meanings of individual scores).

3. Academic Achievement Assessments

These assessments measure a student's academic level in reading, mathematics, written language, social studies and science. Results of these tests are used to determine a student's achievement of school skills as compared to other age or grade level peers.

a. Woodcock-Johnson Psycho-Educational Battery
Revised Tests of Achievement (Part 2)

The Tests of Achievement is the 2nd part of the two part Woodcock Johnson Psycho-Educational Battery Revised. The first part assesses a student's cognitive ability, and is described in the Cognitive Assessments section. Part 2 of this assessment is designed to provide information about four areas of the curriculum: reading, mathematics, written language, and knowledge (social studies, science, and humanities). The standard battery contains 9 subtests, and the supplemental battery contains 5 subtests.

This achievement assessment can adequately assess skills in people ages 2 to 90+, and in grades K-12 and college age. This assessment is quite easy to administer and is designed for use by professionals such as special education teachers who are trained in the administration and interpretation of individual tests. The test is administered using an easel-style notebook for students to look at. The test administrator has a testing protocol to record student's answers.

Results produced by the Woodcock Johnson Test of Achievement can be reported by subtests, academic areas, and by subskills. More than 30 subtest and academic area results are produced, and each result can be expressed in a variety of scores including **Age-Equivalents, Grade-Equivalents, Standard Scores** and **Percentile Ranks.** (See the **Explanation of Test Scores** section on page 55 for clarification of meanings of individual scores).

b. *Wechsler Individual Achievement Test (WIAT)*

This academic achievement test is designed to be administered along with the Wechsler tests of intellectual performance (WISC). The WIAT is a comprehensive individually administered battery for assessing the achievement of children who are in Grades K through 12 and who are ages 5 years to 19 years 11 months old.

The WIAT contains eight subtests. Two subtests assess reading (Basic Reading and Reading Comprehension), two math (Numerical Operations and Mathematics Reasoning), two written language (Spelling and Written Expression), and two oral language (Listening Comprehension and Oral Expression). The WIAT does assess all the achievement areas that are included in the federal definition of a learning disability. Results of this assessment can be easily compared with results from one of Wechsler Individual Ability tests to see if a significant discrepancy exists between the student's ability and achievement scores (which is the definition of a learning disability). The WIAT does not assess science, social studies, or other content subjects; however, it does provide information about oral language, which is rarely assessed by other individual achievement tests.

The WIAT is most often administered by a school psychologist, as the manual does recommend that professionals with graduate-level training in the use of individually administered assessment instruments are qualified to administer the WIAT and interpret the test results. The results of the WIAT are best used to identify curriculum areas where a student is showing significantly poorer performance in relation to his or her age or grade peers.

Results are provided using **Standard Scores, Percentile Ranks, Age-Equivalent,** and **Grade Equivalent** scores for all subtests administered. These same scores are also provided for the 5 composite scores given (Reading, Mathematics, Language, Writing and Total). The Total Composite score reflects all eight subtests combined. (See the **Explanation of Test Scores** section on page 55 for clarification of meanings of individual scores).

c. *Kaufmann Test of Educational Achievement (K-TEA)*

The K-TEA is an individual measure of academic performance for students ages 6 years to 18 years and 11 months old and in grades 1 through 12. There are two forms of the K-TEA, a Brief Form and a Comprehensive Form. The Brief Form takes approximately 15 to 35 minutes to administer and includes three subtests: Mathematics, Reading, and Spelling.

The Comprehensive Form takes twice as long to administer and offers five additional subtests: **1)** Mathematics/Applications, **2)** Reading/Decoding, **3)** Spelling, **4)** Reading/Comprehension, and **5)** Mathematics/Computation.

Results produced from the K-TEA include **Grade-Equivalent Scores**, **Standard Scores,** and **Percentile Rank** for each subtest as well as for the total test score or the "Battery Composite". For each subtest given and for the Total Reading Cluster, **Grade-Equivalent** and **Age-Equivalent** scores are provided as are **Percentile Ranks** and **Standard Scores.** (See the **Explanation of Test Scores** on page 55 for clarification of meanings of individual scores).

4. Math Assessments

a. KeyMath Revised

The KeyMath Revised is an individually administered test designed to provide a comprehensive assessment of a student's understanding and application of important mathematical concepts and skills. This assessment is for students ages 5 through 16 years old and for students in Kindergarten through 9th grade. The test consists of 13 subtests that are organized into three major areas of mathematics: Basic Concepts (foundation knowledge), Operations (computational skills), and Applications in Mathematics (the use of knowledge and computational skills).

The results from the KeyMath-R help evaluators determine the student's current achievement in basic mathematics concepts, computational operations, and applications such as problem solving, estimation, time, money, and measurement. The KeyMath-R is most useful as a screening device to identify possible mathematical strengths and weaknesses. The KeyMath-R requires no special training to be administered. The KeyMath-R manual states that the test can be administered by regular and special education teachers, classroom aides, and other paraprofessionals, as long as the manual is followed. Test result interpretation, however, is best accomplished by professionals with some formal training in interpreting test results.

For each subtest given, results are expressed using both **Percentile Ranks** and **Scaled Scores.** **Grade-Equivalent** and **Age-Equivalent** scores, **Percentile Ranks** and **Standard Scores** are given for the overall total test as well as for the three major areas assessed (Basic Concepts, Operations, and Applications). (See **Explanation of Test Scores** on page 55 for clarification of meanings of individual scores).

b. Test of Mathematical Abilities (TOMA)

The TOMA attempts to assess the attitudes a student might have toward mathematics, the understanding of vocabulary used in mathematical sense, and the understanding of how information about mathematics is used. The TOMA contains five subtests: 1) Attitude toward math, 2) Vocabulary, 3) Computation, 4) General Information, and 5) Story Problems.

No special training is required to administer the TOMA; however, administrators should study the manual prior to administering the TOMA for the first time. Results are provided with both **Scaled Scores** and **Percentile Ranks** or each subtest given. A

Standard Score is used to provide information regarding the total test score or the "Math Quotient" which is derived by combining all subtest resettles. (See **Explanation of Test Scores** on page 55 for clarification of meanings of individual scores).

5. Reading Assessments

a. Woodcock Reading Mastery Tests-Revised (WRMT-R)

The WRMT-R is used to pinpoint students' strengths and weaknesses in the area of reading. There are two forms of the WRMT-R; Form G and Form H. Form G is a complete battery made up of four tests of reading achievement and a readiness section; Form H is a condensed form which contains only alternate forms of the reading achievement tests.

The four subtests common to both forms are *1) Word Identification* (Students are shown individual words and they must pronounce each word.) **2)** *Word Attack* (Students are asked to pronounce nonsense words and syllables.) **3)** *Word Comprehension* (Students are asked to identify antonyms, synonyms and analogies.) and **4)** *Passage Comprehension* (Students are shown a brief passage with one word omitted, the student is asked to supply the missing word.) Form G contains all of the previously mentioned measures as well as three measures of reading readiness which include: *1) Visual-Auditory Learning, 2) Letter Identification and 3) Supplementary Letter Checklist.*

The WRMT-R is designed for students from kindergarten through college, and ages 5-0 through 75+, but young children and non-readers may experience success only on the readiness subtests.

There is no formal training required to administer the WRMT-R, although prior to administering this test for the first time, examiners should study the test manual, administer at least two practice tests, and be observed and evaluated by an experienced examiner.

The results received from the WRMT-R helps educators to determine the student's current levels of achievement in reading readiness, basic reading skills, and comprehension. These results are most useful for identifying areas of strengths and educational needs.

The WRMT-R offers a variety of scores. For each subtest given and for the Total Reading Cluster, **Grade-Equivalent** and **Age-Equivalent** scores are provided as are **Percentile Ranks** and **Standard Scores.** (See **Explanation of Test Scores** on page 55 for clarification of meanings of individual scores).

b. Test of Reading Comprehension (TORC)

The TORC does not attempt to measure all aspects of the reading process. Instead, it emphasizes comprehension skills, silent reading, and knowledge of word meanings.

The TORC contains eight subtests. It is not necessary to administer all eight subtests, however, to receive an index of general reading comprehension ability, the General Comprehension Core should be administered which consists of the following 4 subtests. **1)** *General Vocabulary* (students are presented with 3 words that are related and then is given 4 other words and the student must choose which word best relates to the other 3 words). **2)** *Syntactic Similarities* (students read 5 sentences and chooses 2 that are most similar in meaning). **3)** *Paragraph Reading* (students read 6 - one or two paragraph selections and answer five multiple-choice questions about each). and **4)** *Sentence Sequencing* (five sentences that make up a paragraph are listed in random order. The student's task is to determine the sequence in which the sentences should appear.)

The Diagnostic Supplements are the other four of the eight subtests that can be administered for additional information. The four Diagnostic Supplements are 1) **Mathematics Vocabulary,** 2) **Social Studies Vocabulary,** 3) **Science Vocabulary** and 4) **Reading the Directions of Schoolwork.**

The TORC is designed for students ages 7-0 to 17-11. Student must be able to work independently and read silently. Administration of the TORC requires no special training and is quite easy to administer. Prior to administering the TORC for the first time, the administrator should give at least 3 practice tests.

Results of the TORC are reported with subtest **scaled scores** and then an overall Reading Comprehension Quotient **(Standard Score)** which is indicative of the student's overall skills level in reading comprehension. **Percentile Ranks** are also given for each individual subtest. (See the **Explanation of Test Scores** on page 55 to further understand the meanings of individual scores).

6. Written Language Assessments

a. Test of Written Language-2 (TOWL-2)

The TOWL-2 is designed to identify students who perform significantly more poorly than their peers in written expression and to determine a student's strength and weaknesses in writing. It is also used to provide directions for further educational assistance.

The test has two forms. Each form assesses three components of language *1) the rules for punctuation, capitalization, and spelling,* *2) the use of written grammar and vocabulary; and 3) the conceptual component, which suggests the ability to produce written products that are logical, coherent, and sequenced.* When administering this test, writing is elicited by means of contrived and spontaneous formats. Spontaneous format are assessed when students are asked to produced writing samples.

There are 10 subtests on the TOWL-2. It does require students to have reading and writing skills. During several subtests, student must read the words or sentences that prompt the writing task. This tests can be administered individually or in a group and it is appropriate for student ages 7 years 6 months through 17 years 11 months.

Result for each subtest on the TOWL-2 can be reported through **Percentile Ranks** and **Scaled Scores.** Three global scores: 1) Contrived Writing Quotient, 2) Spontaneous Writing Quotient, and the 3)Overall Written Language Quotient are reported using **Percentile Ranks** and **Standard Scores.** (See the **Explanation of Test Scores** on page 55 to further understand the meanings of individual scores).

7. Oral Language Assessments

a. Test of Language Development - 3, Primary (TOLD-P:3 Primary) Test of Language Development - 3, Intermediate (TOLD-I:3, Intermediate)

The TOLD-3, Primary and Intermediate versions are individually administered tests of oral language. The primary version is used for preschool and early elementary grade children, ages 4 years to 8 years 11 months. The Intermediate version is used for older elementary grade students, ages 8 years 6 months to 12 years 11 months. The TOLD-P:3, Primary consists of seven subtests which assess receptive and expressive phonology, syntax, and semantics skills. TOLD-I:3, Intermediate consists of six subtests which assess receptive and expressive syntax and semantics skills. The purpose of both versions of the TOLD-3 is to identify a student's strengths and weaknesses in oral language development.

In oral language, speech is the expressive component of language, whereas listening skills is the receptive component. **Phonology** focuses on combining the features of sound into significant speech sounds (phonemes). **Syntax** is the ability to form combinations of words into acceptable phrases, clauses, and sentences. **Semantics** is understanding and making sense of the meaning of the words in sentences.

Administration of the TOLD-3, Primary and Intermediate tests is quite easy. Not all subtests are required to be administered in order to get scores. The administrator of the test can select only those subtests that assess specific language ability such as phonology or syntax depending on the student's needs for the assessment

For the TOLD-P:3, Primary, **Percentile ranks** and **Scaled Scores** are available for each of the seven subtests. **Standard Scores** are also provided for six composite areas. The Spoken Language Quotient is a summary of performance on all subtests. The other composite areas are: Listening Quotient, Speaking Quotient and quotients for Semantics, Syntax and Phonology.

For the TOLD-I:3, Intermediate, **Percentile Ranks** and **Scaled Scores** are available for the six subtests. **Standard Scores** are also provided for five composite areas. The Spoken Language Quotient is a summary of the performance on all subtests. The other composite areas for this assessment are: Listening Quotient, Speaking Quotient, Semantics Quotient, and Syntax Quotient. (See the **Explanation of Test Scores** on page 55 to further understand the meanings of individual scores).

b. Clinical Evaluation of Language Fundamentals-Third Ed. (CELF-3)

The CELF-3 is a diagnostic test which contains 11 subtests that assess syntax, semantics, and memory. This assessment is designed for students ages 5 to 16 years 11 months. The battery does provide several measures of receptive and expressive syntax (forming sentences in appropriate order) and semantics (understanding what the words are telling).

Results of the CELF-3 can be provided using individual subtest **Scaled Scores** and three Global **Standard Scores.** The three standard scores are given in the areas of Receptive Language, Expressive Language, and Total Language. An **Age-Equivalent** score is available for the Total Language global score. (See the **Explanation of Test Scores** on page 55 to further understand the meanings of individual scores).

c. Boehm Test of Basic Concepts-Revised (Boehm-R).

The Boehm-R evaluates receptive vocabulary in young school-aged children. It is designed to assess a student's mastery of basic concepts that are both essential to understanding verbal instruction as well as for successful early school achievement. The results of the Boehm-R can be used to identify students with weaknesses in receptive vocabulary and to identify basic concepts that students have not yet mastered. This test can be administered to a group or an individual.

When taking this assessment, students respond to a total of 50 test items. The concepts that are assessed are basic vocabulary words that appear frequently in instructional materials for young school-aged children.

Results of the Boehm-R are expressed as **Percentile Ranks**. (See the **Explanation of Test Scores** on page 55 to further understand the meanings of individual scores).

d. Peabody Picture Vocabulary Test-Third Edition (PPVT-III)

The PPVT-III is an individually administered test of receptive vocabulary designed for ages 2 years 6 months through 40. The administration of this test only requires 10 to 20 minutes. To administer this test, a student is shown a page containing four drawings. The administrator reads a word and the student points to or says the number of the drawing that represents the word. The PPVT-III is quick and easy to administer. This can be utilized as both a test of achievement because it assesses the acquisition of English vocabulary, and an aptitude test because it assesses verbal skills.

The PPVT-III is not divided into subtests and only one result is obtained, a total test performance index. This total can be reported using several types of scores. **Standard Scores** are used as are **Percentile Ranks** and **Age Equivalent Scores.** (See the **Explanation of Test Scores** on page 55 to further understand the meanings of individual scores).

8. Behavioral Assessments

A wide variety of rating scales and checklists are available for assessing a student's behavior in school, at home, and in the community.

a. Behavior Rating Profile (2nd ed.) (BRP-2)

The BRP-2 attempts to provide a comprehensive overview of a student's current behavioral status. It can be utilized for students ages 6 years 6 months to 18 years 6 months or in grades 1 - 12. Information for this assessment can be gathered from four types of infomrants: *1) students themselves, 2) teachers, 3) parents,* and *4) peers.* The student's behavior at home and in school and the student's interpersonal relationships can be assessed.

The BRP-2 consists of four profiles to be used, depending on the person providing the information. There is a **1)** *Student Rating Scale* which is a self-rating scale for the student to complete, **2)** *The Teacher Rating Scale* is completed by a classroom teacher who knows the student well enough to provide accurate information, **3)** *The Parent Rating Scale* is completed by a parent who can provide accurate information regarding the student in the home environment, and finally, **4)** *The Peer Scale* is a sociometric technique used for the student's classmates to answer the questions. The purpose of the BRP-2 is to identify students with possible behavior disorders who may be in need of further assessment.

Results of the BRP-2 are described using **Scaled Scores** and **Percentile Ranks.** Several scores are available, depending on the scales administered. If the student completed the student rating scale, three separate scores are reported: Home, School, and Peer scores. There is one score for each teacher and each parent who rated the student, and also, each sociometric question answered by the student's peers produces a score.

(See the **Explanation of Test Scores** on page 55 to further understand the meanings of individual scores).

b. Behavior Evaluation Scale-2 (BES-2).

The BES-2 is designed to identify strengths and weaknesses in five behavioral domains of students in grades K through 12. There are 76 behavior descriptions in which the informant must rate according to frequency of those behaviors occurring. There are seven frequency rating choices ranging from "never or not observed" to "continuously throughout the day." Those 76 specific behaviors are then divided into the five types of behavior disorders. The five types of behavior disorders described are *1) Learning Problems, 2) Interpersonal Difficulties, 3) Inappropriate Behavior, 4) Unhappiness/Depression,* and *5) Physical Symptoms/Fears.*

It is recommended that teachers observe students for at least one month before completing the rating scale. The informant should be the teacher with primary instructional responsibility for the student, to ensure that precise completion is occurring.

Subscale **Scaled Scores** and **Percentile Ranks** are distributed for the five behavior disorder areas named above. **Standard Scores** and **Percentile Ranks** are used to describe the Overall Behavior Quotient which combines all five subscales for a total behavior score. (See the **Explanation of Test Scores** on page 55 to further understand the meanings of individual scores).

c. Attention Deficit Disorders Evaluation Scale (ADDES) (Home Version and School Version)

The ADDES is a rating scale designed for use with school-aged children and adolescents ages 4 years through 20 years old. Both a school and home version are available and it asks about specific behaviors which reflect inattention, impulsivity, and hyperactivity. The informant is asked to rate each specific behavior according to the frequency with which is occurs. The Likert Scale includes five ratings to choose from *1) does not engage in the behavior, 2) one to several times per month, 3) one to several times per week, 4) one to several times per day, 5) one to several times per hour.*

Two types of results are produced by the ADDES. There are three subscales (Inattentive, Impulsive, and Hyperactive) which receive separate **Scaled Scores**. The overall total scale, which combines the three subscales is described by a **Percentile Rank.** (See the **Explanation of Test Scores** on page 55 to further understand the meanings of individual scores).

d. Self Esteem Index (SEI)

The SEI is a self-report rating scales for student ages 8 years to 18 years 11 months old. It can be administered either individually or to a group. It contains 80 statements that students rate on a Likert Scale rating. The ratings are: *1) always true, 2) usually true, 3) usually false,* or *4) always false.* Each statement fits into one of four self-esteem scales **1) perception of familial acceptance, 2) perception of academic competence, 3) perception of peer popularity,** and **4) perception of personal security**.

Results of the SEI are described through **Scaled Scores** and **Percentile Ranks** for the four self-esteem scales. Scores on the four scales are combined to produce a total test Self-Esteem Quotient. This quotient is provided through a **Percentile Rank** and a

Standard Score. (See the **Explanation of Test Scores** on page 55 to further understand the meanings of individual scores).

e. Conners' Teacher Rating Scale (CTRS) Conners' Parent Rating Scale (CPRS)

The Conners' Rating Scales (both the teacher and parent scales) are measures that have been used for assessing attention-deficit/hyperactivity disorder (ADHD) in children and adolescents. This rating scale can be used to rate the behavior of children ages 3 to 17 years old. There is a long and short form for both the teacher and parent versions.

Results are reported with both **Scaled Scores** and **Percentile Ranks** for the scales.

Explanation of Test Scores

1. Age and Grade Equivalents

These scores express test performance in terms of the familiar units of chronological age or grade in school. For example, a student may receive an age score of 7-6 (7 years, 6 months) on a test or a grade score of 4.5 (4th grade, 5 month). In general, this means that the student performed on this test as if he or she was 7 years, 6 months old or in the 5th month of 4th grade. This is quite easy for parents and teachers to understand; however, they are not the most reliable scores, thus should be used with caution.

2. Percentile Ranks

This represents the percentage of individuals within the norm group who achieved this raw score or a lower one. If a student earns a percentile rank of 62, it can be said that the student performed at a level equal to or greater than 62% of the norm group, and at a level lower than that of the remaining 28% of the norm group.

3. Standard Scores

Standard scores are most often used to report overall test performance. These scores transform the "raw" score into a derived score to a new scale with a set average. Standard scores are useful for comparing the performance of the same student on two different measures. Most norm-referenced standardized tests use the type of standard score where the average score is 100. This means that if a student received a standard score of 100 on the overall test, he or she would be performing at the exact average, as compared to the norm group of the same age. Students receiving other standard scores, when compared to the same age norm group, would be described as:

130 and above	**Above Average**
116 to 129	**High Average**
85 to 115	**AVERAGE**
71 to 84	**Low Average**
70 and below	**Below Average**

4. Scaled Scores

These scores are most frequently used to refer to subtest scores, unlike the overall score that a standard score represents. Most often, scaled scores place the average score being at 10, thus meaning that if a student received a scaled score on a subtest of 10, he or she would be performing at the exact average as compared to the norm group of the same age. Students receiving other scaled scores, when compared to the same age norm group, would be described as:

17 and above	Above Average
14 to 16	High Average
7 to 13	AVERAGE
4 to 6	Low Average
3 and below	Below Average

Examples of Nontraditional Forms of Assessment

1. Use information gathered through the Teacher's Assistance Team (TAT) or other pre-referral activities
2. Observe the student in various learning environments and settings.
3. Gather information by reading the student's cumulative folder.
4. Analyze the student's work samples, including classroom-based assessments.
5. Implement diagnostic teaching methods or other systematic methods of instruction.
6. Interview persons who can provide key information (e.g., student, parent, previous teachers).

Special Education Acronyms and Abbreviations

ADD	Attention Deficit Disorder
ADHD	Attention Deficit Hyperactivity Disorder
BD	Behavior Disorder
BPD	Bronchopulmonary Dysplasia
CF	Cystic Fibrosis
CMV	Cytomegalovirus
CP	Cerebral Palsy
DAPE	Developmental Adapted Physical Education
DD	Developmental Disability
ECSE	Early Childhood Special Education
E/BD	Emotional or Behavioral Disorder
ED	Emotional Disorder
FAPE	Free Appropriate Public Education
FAS	Fetal Alcohol Syndrome
HI	Hearing Impaired
IDT	Interdisciplinary Team
IEP	Individualized Education Plan
IFSP	Individual Family Service Plan
IQ	Intelligence Quotient
LD	Learning Disability
LRE	Least Restrictive Environment
MMMI	Mild - Moderate Mentally Impaired
MSMI	Moderate - Severe Mentally Impaired
MD	Muscular Dystrophy
MS	Multiple Sclerosis
NTD	Neural Tube Defect
OHI	Other Health Impaired
PI	Physically Impaired
SMI	Severely Multiply Impaired
SLD	Specific Learning Disability
SLP	Speech or Language Pathologist
TBI	Traumatic Brain Injury
VI	Visually Impaired

Section III

Curriculum & Behavior Modifications and Adaptations

I. Curriculum Adaptation and Modifications

1. Language Arts Strategies

a. Reading Comprehension Strategies

Good readers can visualize and form an image in their mind to help them understand what they are reading. Poor readers, however, are unable to do this, and thus experience extreme difficulty with understanding what they are reading. These readers are spending their time decoding and sounding out words and then forget to pay attention to what the words are telling them. Graphic organizers, as described below, are visual depictions of the events and happenings in a story. The graphic organizers are used to assist students in comprehending what they read.

1. Story charts or maps.

Identify the characters, setting, problem, sequence of events, and the resolution of conflict of a story read by using charts and maps. Primary grades will use a slightly modified chart compared to the chart used by the upper elementary grade levels. (See examples on pages. 63 and 64)

2. Storyboard.

Divide the chalkboard or a piece of paper into sections (6-8 sections depending on the length of the story). Have the students draw, write, or dictate for the teacher to record the story events in sequence in each box or section. (See example on page 65).

3. Plot profiles.

After reading a book or story, choose a number of events and produce a class graph of which events students found to be the most exciting. Plot on a large graph the majority opinion of the class regarding how exciting each event was. (Have the students show hands or applaud when you mention the part of the story that they thought was most exciting.)

5. Wanted posters.

Have the students create posters by drawing a picture of and writing about identifying characteristics of a character in the book.

6. Venn diagrams.

Use the circular diagram to compare and contrast two similar books, stories, or pieces of literature. Compare two versions of a story, a book with its movie version, or two characters within a book.

7. Character web.

Put the character's name in the center of the web and then have students report traits and descriptions of that character in the outer sections of the web. (See example on page 66)

Story charts/map

Use this chart to identify the different elements of the story you just read.
(For use with upper elementary.)

Title:
Author:
Illustrator:
Characters:
Setting:
Problem:
Solution:

Story charts/map

Use this chart to identify the different elements of the story you just read.
You can draw a picture or write words to describe the elements.
(For use with primary elementary students.)

Title:
Author:
Illustrator:
Characters:
Setting:
Story Summary:

Storyboard

Draw a picture of, or write a sentence about the story events in the order in which they occurred.

Story Title: Author: Illustrator:	
1.	2.
3.	4.
5.	6.

Character Web

Put the character's name in the center of the web and then write traits and descriptions of that character in the outer sections of the web.

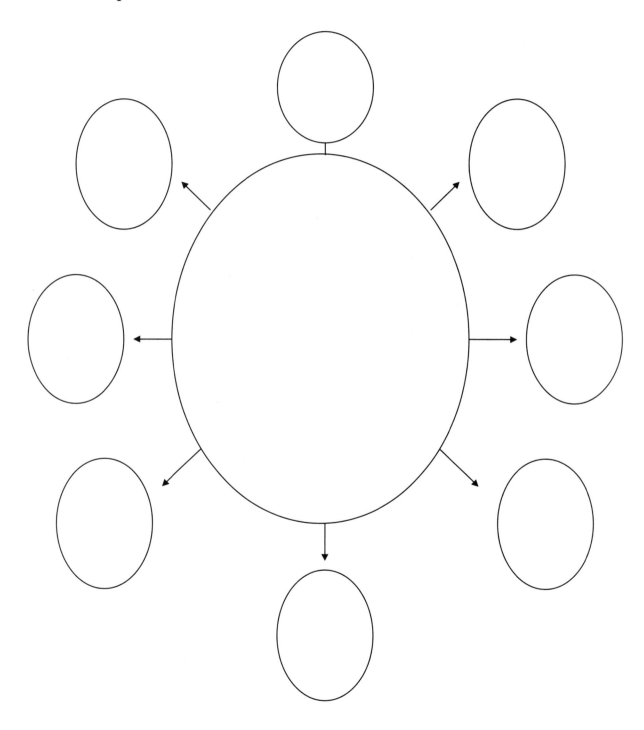

b. Oral Reading Strategies

Students who have difficulty reading, also have a hard time following along and paying attention. These students frequently lose their place in the passage, and thus receive no meaning out of the words they are reading. In many cases, students with poor oral reading skills are so scared of the embarrassment they think they will experience if they have to read orally, that they are only concerned with the short passage that they will be expected to read and thus lose the meaning in whole passage. Here are some oral reading strategies to try in order to avoid frustration and panic from those who struggle with reading orally.

1. Teacher read out loud.

You orally read the story first, modeling for fluency, expression, and interest while the students are following along with their own copy of the selection (require younger students point to each word that you are reading).

2. Read silently before orally.

Give the students a chance to first read the selection silently before being asked to read orally. Students who are uncomfortable reading orally (particularly older students) should never be forced to read out loud to the class. They should be able to volunteer when they wish to read in front of the class. Buddy reading or reading is small groups rather than in front of the whole class is a much "safer," preferable way for students to practice their oral reading.

3. Utilize volunteers or student aides to assist children with reading.

Have student aides or volunteers (parents, grandparents, etc.) listen to the children read. Provide a brief inservice for volunteers who will be listening to students read in order to inform them of how best to provide assistance.

4. Buddy or partner reading.

Assign a reading buddy or partner for each student. It is beneficial to strategically place more confident readers with those who struggle. Before attempting to partner read for the first time, explain to students that they are to be helpful to their buddies, but that the partner should not just read the selection for the student who may be struggling.

Give each student a chance to read the story individually at first, explain that the partners will take turns reading orally and listening to their buddy read. Explain in advance how much a student is to read before the partner begins reading. When possible, allow students to share one book; however, if this is not beneficial for distractible students, it may be better for each student to use his or her own copy of the book.

Buddies can take turns or can read in unison. You can assign questions to the pair of students, so they know what they will have to answer once they have read the story. This helps to provide the group with a purpose for reading. Allow students their own space in which to read, so they are not distracted by other groups.

c. Spelling Strategies.

Many students are poor spellers for many reasons. These students are often inattentive to visual detail, and struggle to recall the letters and word spellings. They often are not visually aware of patterns in words and are careless in their writing and spelling. Here are some ways that may help with students learning to spell.

Strategies for practicing spelling words.

1. Teach high-frequency words.

High frequency words should be top priority in your spelling instruction. One thousand words account for over 90% of the words that are most frequently used in everyday writing.

2. Have the students write the words in the air, using large movements.

Have student say the letters out loud as they write them in the air.

3. Write words in glue or starch on a piece of cardboard.

Then sprinkle glitter, sand, salt, or any powdery material over the top of the glue or starch. Once it dries, it creates a textured, 3-D spelling word which can be used for tactile practice of tracing the words.

4. Give each student a tray of sand or salt.

Have students write the spelling words with their finger in the sand or salt while spelling out loud.

5. Fingerpaint spelling words.

Use shaving cream on the desktop for student to practice writing words. Also try spreading a small amount of pudding or frosting on a paper plate and having students their write words with their finger. Once the word is written, the student can erase it by smoothing the shaving cream, or frosting and then can write the next word.

6. Pair students.

Have them write use their fingers to trace their spelling words on their partners back or they can orally spell the words back and forth between partners.

7. Use individual chalkboards or whiteboards.

Supply colored chalk for chalkboards or colored pens for whiteboards. This can work for a whole group activity, once the spelling words are writen, on the count of three, have the students hold up the boards for you to do a quick check of the words.

8. Dip a clean paintbrush in water.

Have students practice writing words on the chalkboard or desktop.

9. Use manipulative letters.

Provide students with magnetic letters, alphabet cookies, sponge letters, rubber stamps, or stencils to use for individual practice of the words.

10. Play games.

Have oral drills, or spelling bees.

11. Practice typing words on a computer.

12. Use configuration clues.

Print a word and then outline its shape in a different color. This will help students to recognize the use of tall letters and letters which go below the bottom line.

Strategies for testing spelling skills

1. Pronounce each word slowly.

Slowly say the individual sounds of each word when dictating the spelling words. This helps students hear the sequence of the sounds as they spell.

2. Provide adequate time.

Give students the time they need to get the word down carefully before going on to the next word. Also, give additional time after the test to go over and finish writing words that weren't completed at first.

3. Provide shortened spelling lists.

(For students who have significant difficulty in this skill.) Provide "extra credit" for any words beyond the shortened list that students may study for and attempt to spell during a test.

4. Allow students to take tests orally.

Have students take a written test and an oral test. Use whichever score is higher.

d. Handwriting Strategies

Some students often have trouble writing neatly on and within the given lines of a piece of paper. They often form their letters incorrectly and their written work may look disorganized and sloppy. Many students write so quickly causing their handwriting to be unreadable. Others, however, write extremely slow to produce their best work, however, it takes too much time during the day to complete an assignment. It is found that quite often, the cause of many students incorrect handwriting practices is that in the lower grades where proper letter formation strokes were taught, these students were either inattentive or not understanding of what was being taught, thus, they created their own unique way of forming letters. Unfortunately, once letters are learned incorrectly, it is almost impossible to break students of these habits. Once a student has found his or her own way of writing, it will become permanent. This emphasizes the importance of consistent and correct teaching in the early, primary school years. If you have a student struggling with handwriting difficulties, try some of the following suggestions.

1. Carefully teach and model new letters on an overhead projector chalkboard.

Show the strokes as you talk through the steps of forming the letters.

2. Demonstrate letters using large movements in the air.

Talk through the strokes and formation of the letters as you practice writing the letters in the air. Have student write the letters in the air also. Watch each student to ensure that each is making the correct stokes.

3. Consistently require students to correct mistaken letters in all written work.

Bring student's attention to letter reversals and misformed letters in all assignments. Assist students in correcting their mistakes.

4. Always observe while students are practicing.

Walk around the room to try and identify students who are in need of one-on-one or small group assistance or those who need immediate re-teaching. Once a student learns incorrectly to write letters, it is almost impossible to break them of that habit.

5. Provide students with pencil grips or thick pencils.

This will help them to have a bit more control over the movement of their pencils.

e. Written Expression Strategies

Writing is very difficult for many students, especially when they are expected to "just write". For many, determining a topic about which to write and then gathering ideas about that topic is very troublesome. These students struggle to place their ideas on paper in an interesting and descriptive way. Here are some strategies to try with kids who have difficulty with this in your class.

1. Develop a list of topics of interest.

As a class, brainstorm a list of topics that would be of interest for most students to write about. Some examples may be sports, scary things, vacation places, or favorite things to do at home. This becomes a class list that can be posted in the classroom and then serves as a idea generator when students are expected to write in journals or any other writing activity. When students say "I don't know what to write about" you can direct them to the list.

2. Semantic mapping.

This strategy helps students to organize their thoughts before they begin writing. Place the main topic in the center of the paper. Place subcategories around the main topic and then add details pertaining to the subcategories.

3. Give alternatives to over-used words.

Generate a class word list or word bank of over-used, boring words (1-cent words) that can be substituted for more interesting words (10-cent words and 25-cent words). Use a thesaurus to have students find "more valuable" words.

1-Cent	10-cents	25-cents
run	race	sprint
	dash	scramble
	speed	hasten
fast	hasty	swift
		speedy

4. Teach descriptive language.

Post examples of metaphors, similies and other examples of descriptive language found in literature. Encourage students to find examples or descriptive language in their reading. Provide time during each week for students to share the examples that they have found.

5. Show - not tell.

Teach students to create a picture or scene using words.

A. Have students close their eyes and ask them to think of a scene or picture with which they are familiar. Have students, orally at first, and then in writing, describe what the scene or picture, feels like, tastes like, looks like and sounds like. Encourage students to think about all of their senses to assist them in writing descriptively.

B. Have students chose a picture (a photograph, magazine picture, postcard, or illustration of a story). Have each student write a descriptive paragraph about his or her chosen picture. Display all pictures used, around the classroom. Randomly pass out the paragraphs to all students. Have each student read their given paragraph and then try to match the paragraph with the picture that was described.

6. Keep a writing folder for all students

Each student should have a writing folder available for personal use to write down thoughts or ideas. These thoughts or ideas could later be used for topic ideas or free write ideas during later assignments.

7. Pen Pals.

Arrange opportunities with other teachers and classrooms for students to write notes or letters to students in other classrooms within the same school or in different schools.

8. Daily Journals.

Students need daily opportunities to practice writing, not to be graded on, but to practice writing for fluency and consistency. It is best to have a specific period of time on a daily basis for journal writing. It may be necessary and beneficial to provide sentence starters or journal prompts for those who find it difficult to independently choose a topic.

9. Buddy journals.

Provide each of your students with a writing buddy from either their same classroom or from a different section of that grade level. The writing buddies will utilize the journal as a way to converse with each other through reading and writing. One buddy will write something and the other buddy will read it and respond to what was written.

f. Written Mechanics Strategies

Students who struggle academically are often very weak in language mechanics. They struggle to seek and find their own errors and to self correct their written work. Try some of these strategies with students who struggle with the mechanics of writing.

1. Provide frequent reminders

Students need to be reminded frequently to check their work for capitalization and punctuation errors.

2. Use questioning techniques to help students find their own errors.

Teacher - "What two things do all sentences need?"
Student - "A capital letter at the beginning and an end mark at the end."
Teacher - "Does your sentence have both of those things?"

3. Frequently model how to edit and find mechanical errors.

Provide students with examples of work with mechanical errors. As a class, correct the errors by walking through the passage step by step. Be sure to explain why the specific examples are erroneous.

4. Let students edit each other's work.

This work well, as students are often more observant with other's work than with their own.

5. Dictate to students.

Provide one or two sentences orally to students for them to write. Provide reminders for students to check the beginning and ending of the sentence. Write the sentence correctly on the overhead or board and have students check their work. Ask the students "Do your sentences look like mine?"

6. Have the student dictate a few sentences.

Copy exactly what the student says onto a chart. Be sure that all students are watching as you are writing what is being said. As you record what the student is telling you, "forget" to add punctuation and capitalization to the sentences. Have students identify where the errors in the sentences. Always require students to explain why the corrections must be made. Continually repeating the rules of written mechanics will help students to become more familiar with them in their own writing.

2. Math Strategies

Many students who typically struggle with academic requirements in school, have exhibited learning strengths in spatial awareness, logical thinking, reasoning, and visualization. They have the ability to excel in a balanced mathematics curriculum which emphasizes patterns, geometry, measurement, probability, and logic. These students need hands-on activities and do benefit from the use of manipulatives (pattern blocks, base-ten blocks, interlocking cubes, cubes, and tiles) graphing activities, searching for patterns, and other nontextbook, nonsworksheet type strategies. It is important that the emphasis of teaching mathematics is not by assigning students problem after problem, page after page of tedious computation.

Computation Strategies

1. Allow extra time on written math tests.
This will allow for students experiencing difficulty to not feel the need to rush, thus making careless errors.

2. Provide cubes, buttons, counters or other manipulatives.
Allow children to utilize materials that will assist them in their problem solving process.

3. Provide "Touch Math" strategies.
Offer this strategy, as a supplement to your regular mathematics instruction, for students to use if they choose, in order to assist with adding on and counting back. Touch math helps students to strategically place touch points on the numbers 0 - 9 and then use the numbers by touching and counting on or counting back.

4. Permit and encourage the use of calculators.
If students are struggling with the computational aspects, allow them to use calculators.

5. Provide them with an option of paper.
When students are working on problems which require them to show their work, allow them to record their work (a) on regular paper with two or three lines of space between problems, (b) on lined notebook paper, turned sideways, or (c) on wide width graph paper.

6. Assign an appropriate number of problems.
In an attempt to determine if a student grasps a specific mathematical concept, or to provide practice on the concept, there is no purpose in assigning all 25 - 30 problems frequently placed on a math worksheet. If a student can do 8 or 9 of the problems correctly, it is safe to assume that the student has grasped the concept.

7. *Avoid stress of timed tests of basic facts.*

Many student struggle with memorizing the basic addition, subtraction, multiplication and division basic facts. Often times, when given time to think, these students are well aware of the answers to the basic fact problems, however, the essence of the "timed test" contributes anxiety, causing the student to perform poorly on the timed test. Expect students to complete the same test, however, do not require it to be completed in a certain amount of time. Also, give credit to the student for being able to respond orally, or if some students need to rely on manipulatives, don't penalize them. Students are learning, if they know the process in which to reach the answer of a mathematical problem. The length of time it takes to get through that process should not penalize the student.

8. *Reduce the amount of copying.*

Provide students who struggle with photocopied pages of assignments. Allow another person (aide, parent, volunteer) to help the student by copying the problems onto paper for that student.

9. *Highlight processing signs.*

This will draw attention to which operation is necessary for successful compleion of the problem. Many students tend to be not attentive to operations signs on a page, especially if they change frequently (from + to -, for example).

10. *Color or highlight the ones column.*

Draw attention to where the student is supposed to begin working on the problem.

11. *Provide students with only one worksheet at a time.*

Avoid overwhelming students with too many pages at one time.

12. *Visually list all steps for each process.*

Write the steps for the different mathematical processes and have them posted throughout the room for students to refer to when needed.

13. *Use whiteboards and overhead projectors for teaching mathematical concepts.*

Utilize overhead, transparencies, manipulatives like calculators, pattern blocks, cubes, etc. in daily teaching. Students often grasp materials when they can visually see as well as hear how to work through a specific process.

3. Test Strategies

a. Test Taking (for students)

The word "TEST" causes extreme anxiety for many students, especially those who struggle with academic requirements and is quite frequently a very frustrating and unsuccessful experience. Here are some important suggestions to help students become more comfortable with their test-taking skills. Spend a few days teaching these skills to the student before the test to allow them to become comfortable and knowledgeable about them.

Teach students to first recognize what kinds of formats are being used on the tests. Many times, more than one format is used throughout a test. Once the format is determined, the following steps will assist you in answering the questions as accurately as possible.

I. Multiple Choice Formats.

1. Read through the question. Try to answer to the question, if possible, before reading the multiple choices given.

2. If you are able to answer the question, then read through the choices and find the answer that closely parallels your answer.

3. If you are unsure of the answer to that question, move on to the next question. Do not spend time at the beginning of the test attempting to answer questions of which you are unsure.

4. Once you have answered the questions that you are sure of, go back to answer the rest of the questions.

5. When answering a question that you are unsure of the answer, look through the choices given. Cross out the obvious incorrect answers. Try to eliminate at least 2 answers so that you only have 2 answers to choose from.

6. Once you have narrowed your choices to 2 answers and if you are still uncertain, make a guess that would make the best sense to you.

II. Matching Formats.

1. Read through both columns of information completely before attempting to make any matches.

2. Answer the items that you are sure of by matching those first.

3. Cross out all choices once you have used them. (Be certain that the answers are only going to be used one time each before crossing them out.)

4.   Once you have made all matches that you are certain of, and crossed out all coordinating matches, go back to complete all remaining matches.

5.   If you are uncertain of which matches to make of the remaining choices, make a choice that would make the best sense to you.

6.   After all mathces are made, go back and check to be sure that you have used all matching choices from both columns.

III. Fill in the Blank Formats.

1.   Read through all the questions first. Answer all questions that you are confident of first. If a word bank is provided, cross out answers that you have used.

2.   Use only key words in the blank.

3.   Once you have answered all questions that you are sure of, refer to other items in the test to see if they will provide you with useful information to assist in answering the other questions.

4.   If you are uncertain of the answer, make a choice that would make the best sense to you.

IV. Essay Formats.

1.   Read all of the essay questions entirely before attempting to answer any of the essay questions.

2.   Once you have read all essay questions, choose the easiest one to answer.

3.   Once you have chosen which one to answer first, write down all facts that you feel are essential to know when answering the question. Put the facts in an order that will assist you in answering the question. Use the written facts to help you write the essay.

4.   After completing the question, re-read it carefully to be sure that what you have written aligns with what the question is asking for. Be sure that you have answered all parts of the question.

b. Test Writing (for teachers)

I. Before the test.

1. *Allow time in class to review.* Provide a test study guide for students. Allow time during the class prior to the test to review the information on the study guide. Provide games or activities for students to participate in to help them study the information that will be on the test.

2. *Provide a review test.* This is essential, especially if students are unfamiliar with the format of the test. Students need practice on multiple choice, fill-in-the-blank, matching and essays formats. They also need to know what the teacher is going to expect from them. Allow students to take the study guide home 2 or 3 nights before the test in order to study at home as well.

II. The Test.

1. *Organize and format the test carefully.* Be sure that the test is written so all children can read it. Most students are able to read typed print, however, if you are unable to type it, be sure to print it. Do not write a test in cursive, as not all students can read cursive handwriting. Be sure that adequate white space is left on the paper. Tests which seem to have test items crowded onto a page will seem very overwhelming to many students. Two pages with appropriately spaced questions will seem much less intimidating for students than one page with very little white space.

2. *Allow students to respond orally*, if a student feels more comfortably doing so. Either have the student read the answers to a paraprofessional or aide, or have the students read the answers into a tape recorder. If time is available, the student could read directly to the teacher as well. A teacher will receive much better information regarding what a student actually knows, if the students struggles with writing but is allowed to respond orally.

3. *Allow the test to be read to the student.* If a student struggles with reading decoding, but understands the conceptual material being assessed on the test, the teacher will get a much more accurate assessment of the student's knowledge if the test is read to the student.

4. *Provide shortened tests.* This should be used only for students who will become overwhelmed by longer tests.

5. *Be sure that students are understanding what the test is asking them to do.* Make yourself available during the test to answer student's questions about the test.

II. Behavior Management Intervention Strategies

1. Transition Times

Transition times and non-instructional times of the day are often the most challenging times for many students. Here are some ways to help avoid behavior difficulties during those times.

1. Inform students of any upcoming changes occurring in the daily schedule.

Try to avoid any surprises in the routine. If there is an assembly, guest speaker, substitute teacher, or any other changes, inform students of this prior to the change occurring.

2. Discuss what will happen and teach the specific behaviors that are required for each new situation.

Use techniques such as role-playing and practicing of the specific behaviors before introducing a new situation to the students.

3. Use flashing lights, ringing of a bell, or some sort of a cue to inform the children that an activity will soon be ending.

Be consistent with the cues you use so that children are familiar with the cue you use and always know what it means when you utilize that cue. Five or two minute warnings work great for children, as it forwarns them of the upcoming conclusion to a project.

4. Allow "down time" or a couple of minutes of rest time, or exercise time between activities.

This will help students to get some of their "wiggles" out before moving on to the next activity.

5. Be prepared to physically help a child through a transition time.

This is very helpful for the child who struggles to go through a transition time appropriately. Close proximity to that child will often be very beneficial and serve as a reminder for that child to remain "in control."

6. *Provide whole class incentives for smooth transitions.*

There are a variety of ways to do this. One way would be to provide the class with 1 point, every time a transition is handled smoothly. Once the class reaches 10 points, they have earned a popcorn party, or free time, or outside time. Another way would be to place a circle on the chalkboard. For every smooth transition, a check mark is placed inside the circle. When 10 (or whatever number you feel is appropriate) is reached and whole class reward is given.

2. Attention

a. Getting it

1. Provide a signal to get student's attention.

Turn off or flash the lights, ring a bell, or clap or raise your hand to signal the students to turn their attention toward you.

2. Use different tones and volumes of your voice.

Use loud, soft, and whispering voices. Try using a consistent chant or action to get attention "Clap once" (children clap once), "Clap twice" (children clap twice). Children should know that voices should be off after clapping twice. Once there has been silence, you can continue in a normal voice to give directions.

3. Eye contact.

Always ensure that you have all student's eye contact before giving any instructions. Student must know that if they are in a position where they cannot gain eye contact with the teacher, they need to move so that they can have eye contact. This is something that must be taught to the students. For example, if a student's back is to the teacher from where he or she is sitting, teach the student to always turn his or her chair for the time that instructions are being given so that he or she can see the teacher.

4. Always show excitement and enthusiasm about the lessons and activities that are being taught.

If students see that you are excited about what is upcoming, they tend to become interested and excited as well.

5. Do what it takes to get attention, even if it means being silly.

Sometimes using props, or dressing up is an easy way to get the students attention and interest about the upcoming lesson.

6. Be Mysterious.

Inside a box or bag, place an item that is related to the upcoming lesson. Show students the box or bag and encourage them to guess or predict what they think is inside the box or bag. This will keep their excitement and interest about the upcoming lesson.

b. Maintaining It

1. Use visualization.
Write important, key information on the board or on transparencies on an overhead.

2. Be colorful.
Use colored chalk or pens to highlight information or key points on the chalkboard or overhead. Write individual steps to mathematical problems, vocabulary or key words, spelling words, phonics rules, and so on in different colors.

3. Draw student's attention to important information
Frame it with a colored box or square or with your hands.

4. Use your finger, pointing stick, knitting needle, or conductor's baton
Pointing to pertinant information. This will help to focus the students attention on the important information. (Overhead projectors are a great way to focus your students' attention. The overhead projector allows you to write down the important information in color, but allows you to face the students while doing so. It is unlike writing on a chalk board, where you must turn your back on the students. The overhead projector improves classroom management by helping to reduce behavior problems. Students enjoy participating in activities which use the overhead projector.)

5. Use a flashlight or a lighted pointer.
It is very easy to gain student's attention when the lights are turned off and a flashlight or lighted pointer is used to highlight important information.

6. Utilize hands on materials and activities whenever possible.
Be sure and involve students in their learning whenever appropriate.

7. Use a pleasant, but firm voice.
Be sure that you can be clearly heard by all students.

8. Keep the lesson easily understandable.
Teach lessons at a quick pace, yet be sure that student's are understanding each step.

9. Be prepared.
If you are prepared for each lesson beforehand, this will reduce the amount or down time that students will have.

10. Have students record important information.

Have student take brief notes about what has been taught.

11. Call on students with equity.

Teachers tend to unintentionally ignore or refrain from calling on certain students in the classroom. Most often, teachers are generally unaware that they overlook certain students in the classroom. Some times, the will more frequently call on females than males or vice versa. Some teachers tend to call on students who will most likely provide the correct information. Other teachers will purposefully call on students who they think are unsure of the answer or who have not been paying attention. Most often, students are very keen on this and quickly learn their teachers' habits and can often predict their chances of being called on. Students who perceive that they will be required to contribute and speak in front of their peers will remain more attentive.

Try some of these suggestions to assist with greater equity:

a.- Have each student's name written on a card. When it comes time to call on students to answer a question, pull a name from the deck of cards and call on that student. Replace the card back into the deck, making it possible for that student to be called upon again.

b.- Write the students' names on popsicle sticks, place the sticks in a cup and when needed, pull the sticks at random to call on students. Place the stick back into the cup, making it possible for that student to be called upon again.

c.- Have students self-record their opportunities of being chosen to answer a question. Tell students that you are trying to become more consistent in calling on all student's names and that every time you call on them, they should make a tally mark on their card. This can be done for any amount of time. At the end of the predetermined time, collect the cards to evaluate your pattern of students selection.

12. Wait, wait, wait!

Wait at least 5 seconds before moving on to a new student to answer a question. This may seem like forever, but it is true that it takes many students more time to process the question, gather their thoughts, and then express their answer. While standing and waiting for a student to answer, slowly count to 5 before rephrasing the question or moving on.

13. Allow special circumstances.

Be sensitive to students who are often viewed by peers as poor students who never know the answer. Be willing to make a deal with these students in order for them to feel more comfortable with answering questions in front of the whole class. Tell the student to and raise his or her hand with a fist closed, or first finger pointing up, and then you will know not to call on that student for that question. Then when the student is quite certain of the answer to a question, he or she can raise an open hand and you will call on him or her on those occasions.

Ways for whole group response:

Periodically check for understanding of concepts by using whole group response methods. Whole group responses do not give students a chance to "zone out" or become off task during the questions and answer part of a lesson.

1. Use individual whiteboards or chalkboards.

Each student has one at his or her desk. Have students write the answer to your question on the whiteboard. On the count of 3, each student holds up his or her board under his or her chin. This allows the teacher a quick view of the answer and can also determine which students are understanding the concept and which students need remediation.

2. Telling the answer in unison.

Hold up your open hand to students while you are asking the question. This means that student are to be listening and not speaking. Once you have asked the question, give some "think time" for students to process the question. On the count of three close your hand to a fist which signals the students to call out the answer at the same time.

3. Point/tap method.

When drilling students on reading new spelling or vocabulary words, tell the students that whenever you are pointing to the left of a word, they need to be trying to read the word silently. The students should know then that when you point to the word with your pointer, chalk, light or finger, they are to say the word out loud, in unison. Be sure and give some "think time" before pointing to the word and asking for a unison response.

4. Yes/No whole class responses.

These can be done in a variety of ways. The most effective way of yes/no whole class response is through hand signals or colored cards. When hand signals or card are used, these responses should take place right by the chin and close to the body so no other student can see what their neighbor is doing. that there is communication only between the teacher and individual students.
Examples may include:
    a.- Thumbs up / Thumbs down
    b.- Open hand / Closed hand
    c.- Red card / Green card
    d.- Happy face / Sad face card
    e.- Lead end / Eraser end (of a pencil)

3. Keeping Students On Task

1. Continually check for understanding.
Before asking student to work independently, be sure that all directions are understood and clear.

2. Give a manageable amount of work.
Be sure that the amount of work given to a student is not too demanding and overwhelming. This may not mean the same amount of work for each student, as some students are able to do more independently seat work than others.

3. Model and reinforce on-task behavior.
Always define the on-task behavior during reinforcement ("I like the way John is sitting quietly at his desk and working on his assignment".)

4. Set a time amount.
This will work well for those students who enjoy the challenge of a "Beat the clock" system for getting work done. This is neither effective nor appropriate for all students.

5. Put students who model appropriate, on-task behavior in the proximity of the student who struggles to remain on task.
This helps for students to see good modeling and will also reduce the chances of other student's encouraging inappropriate behaviors

6. Provide a quiet study space.
A study carrel works well for the student who is easily distracted by objects, noises, movement, and events. Try providing the student with a headset (with or without music playing), in order to decrease the noises that may be distracting.

7. Use contracts, behavior charts, or other behavior modification systems.
This works well to encourage on-task behavior.

8. Use response costs and naturally occurring consequences.
This works well for off-task behavior. If students are off-task during class time, they can "owe you time" at the end of the day, before school, or for part of recess time. The student must repay the amount of time that he or she was not on task during work time.

9. Signals or colored signs indicating "I need help!"
Some teachers use a signal (thumbs up, or head on desk), or a colored sign that students may place on their desks to alert any adult scanning the room that he or she needs help.

4. Organization

a. Homework

1. Assign a peer study buddy to assist the student.

This can be beneficial both for the student requiring the assistance as well as for the peer who is providing the assistance. Be sure that the assigned buddy is one that will work well with this student. This study buddy can help the student to record homework assignments in a notebook or to be sure that the assignments are completed correctly.

2. Give written assignments.

Don't just provide student with oral assignments. When you are writing the assignment information on the board or overhead projector, have students record their assignments in their assignment notebooks atthe same time.

3. Take a couple of minutes at the end of every day to review student's homework for that night.

Check to ensure that all students have the appropriate books and school materials going home in order to complete the homework assignments.

4. Let parents know when students are struggling with homework requirments.

5. Be specific about your expectations for being prepared for class

When students come to class unprepared, give them inferior, less desirable materials as substitution (backside of ditto paper, old, chewed up pencils.) Do not allow them to go and get their forgotten materials and do not allow them to borrow from a neighbor. They need to know that you are serious about your expectations.

6. Check notebooks often.

Reward students for good organization (e.g., special certificates, "no homework tonight" passes, special privileges). Have routine checks as well as unannounced checks of notebooks.

7. Collect all homework.

Have a specific place for turning assignments in each day, have a teacher's helper collect the homework, or go student to student and personally collect it. Be sure that student's know that you will be checking it and providing accountability for completed homework.

8. Make sure homework is review or practice work.

Do not assign anything new that the student will struggle to complete.

9. Listen to comments from parents and students regarding homework completion.

If a parent is concerned because his or her child is spending many hours each night on homework, consider modifying the requirements and reducing the workload.

10. Color code textbooks, notebooks and folders.

Color coordinate each subject. For example, the blue science book goes with the blue notebook and blue folder.

11. Provide organizational tools.

Allow students to use a pre-made daily assignment sheet or an organizational materials card to serve as visual reminders for what they are required to complete. (See examples on pages 88 and 89)

Organizational Card

(This can be adapted to meet the needs of your particular student, here are two examples)

Name _____

Did I remember?

	Binder	Books	Materials	Teacher's Initials
Monday				
Tuesday				
Wednesday				
Thursday				
Friday				
Point Total				

Did I remember?

	Pencil	Paper	Book	Teacher's Initials
Monday				
Tuesday				
Wednesday				
Thursday				
Friday				
Point Total				

Daily Assignments

Name_____

Date _____

Subject	Assignment	Done	Homework	Done
		☐ Yes ☐ No		☐ Yes ☐ No
		☐ Yes ☐ No		☐ Yes ☐ No
		☐ Yes ☐ No		☐ Yes ☐ No
		☐ Yes ☐ No		☐ Yes ☐ No
		☐ Yes ☐ No		☐ Yes ☐ No
		☐ Yes ☐ No		☐ Yes ☐ No

b. Written work organization

1. Teach consistent ways to complete the work.

Teach the students what you expect their work to look like. Require that all work be written on notebook paper, skipping every other line. Insist that the student's name, the date, the subject, and page number must be written on every assignment on the upper portion of the page. (Have a poster posted at the front of the classroom with the appropriate way to label a notebook page for an assignment, for students to refer to.) Once a specific standard is established, require this of every assignment.

2. Teach students to provide appropriate spacing and avoid crowding on the paper.

Teach students to place "2 finger spaces" between each word to avoid crowding.

3. Lightly draw in left and right margins on paper.

This will help students to learn not to cross the boundary lines.

4. Use heavier, thicker paper that doesn't rip easily.

This will help so that the student's frequent erasures does not result in a torn paper.

5. Teach letter sizes for handwriting.

Refer to the top line as a "head line", middle line as the "belt line," and the bottom line as a "foot line." When writing letters, such as the letter "b" remind students to start at the head line, go all the way down to the foot line and add a belly at the middle line.

6. Organization of math problems on a notebook page.

Encourage students to leave lots of space between problems, even if this means using more pieces of paper. It can also be helpful to have students use graph paper for math computation problems. (Write one number in each section of the graph paper. This will help the student keep track of the place value columns.) Or, encourage students to use regular notebook paper turned sideways with lines going up and down the page, rather than across the page. This will help students keep their columns aligned properly.

			4	7	2
3		+		2	2
			4	9	4

c. Time Management

1. Help with independent time management and organization.

Put a clock face or faces on a students' desks. Set the clock so that the hands are pointing to the time that the individual student needs to leave the room for various pull-out services. Also write time in words and numbers as an extra reminder. Encourage students to remember, on their own, when the time is to leave the room.

2. Make daily schedules.

Tape the schedules to each student's desk to assist with remembering the different events occurring during the day.

3. Use a 10 or 15-minute time period system *(or whatever time period is adequate)*.

Set the time for an appropriate amount of time you expect an assignment to take a student to complete (it should no exceed 15 - 20 mintes). If the assignment is completed with accuracy within that time frame, the teacher provides a reinforcer.

d. Parental Help with Organization

1. Provide a work place free of distractions and away from the TV.

2. Provide appropriate materials necessary for completing homework.

3. Consistently check your child's assignment notebook.

This works best if this is done at the same time and place each night. For example, your child should know to place his or her assignment notebook on the kitchen table as soon as he or she gets home from school, as you will check it right before supper every night.

4. Help your child to prioritize his or her "to do" list each night.

5. Develop and enforce a consistent routine or schedule.

A sample schedule might involve, snack, homework, dinner, play, wind down, bedtime.

6. Help your child pack his or her backpack for the next day.

Make sure that all needed materials for school are in the backpack. It is best to do this before going to bed at night rather than the next morning, as mornings can be hurried.

5. Strategies for Giving Directions

Make sure that the directions you give are clear, concise and understood by all of your students. The following strategies will help to ensure that your students can successfully follow your directions.

1. Wait until you have everyone's attention.
Wait until all students are completely quiet. You may need to provide certain cues to alert students and remind them to maintain their focus.

2. Explain your expectations as clearly as possible.
Take your time when giving directions, as the extra time spent will be beneficial in the end. Be sure that all students can see you when you are providing the instructions. Sometimes students pick up cues from your body language.

3. Provide instructions for all learning styles.
Provide visual and verbal instructions. Write the instructions on the board or overhead while you are giving them orally. Leave the written instructions visual while students are completing the assignment.

4. Show the class what they are to do.
Do not just verbally "tell" the class, but show them as well.

5. Explain each step of the directions slowly and concisely.

6. Have students record assignment due dates in their assignment notebooks.
Leave the assignment written on the board until the end of the day.

7. Always check for understanding.
Ask for specifics
Teacher: "What problems do we need to do"
Class: "Only the odd numbers"

8. Have students repeat the directions back to you before they begin working on the assignment.

9. Give complete directions.
Be sure to explain what students are expected to do when they complete the task.

6. Behavioral Interventions

1. Explain your expectations and requirements.
Make sure that students understand what you are asking of them.

2. Directly teach students what is acceptable and unacceptable.
This needs to be taught for all areas of the school. The classroom, hallway, bathroom, lunchroom, computer room, recess, etc. Provide reinforcement for acceptable behavior and consequences for unacceptable behavior.

3. Provide structure, routine, predictability, and consistency.
This is true for in the classroom as well as in other areas of the school.

4. Allow practice, appropriate modeling, and review of behavioral expectation and rules.

5. Provide clear and fair consequences for all students.

6. Follow-through each and every time.
If a student does not follow a specific rrule, provide consequences every time. Students need to know that you are serious.

7. Use proactive tactics rather than reactive.
Utilizing proactive, reinforcements will minimize the need for reactive consequences.

8. Keep a structured classroom.
Students must know exactly what is expected of them in your classroom at all times.

Behavioral problems often occur when students are undirected and during unstructured times of the day. Planning well and beginning instruction promptly are generally good deterrents to behavior problems. When coming into the classroom from transition times such as at the start of the day, after recess, after physical education., hand the students a brief assignment to work on as they enter to room. This ensures that the students have something to work on until you are ready to begin the next activity.

Here are some ways to avoid significant, behavioral outbreaks by students.

a. Positive Reinforcement

Positive reinforcement is the best, least restrictive, behavioral management strategy that can be used in the classroom at all times. Positive reinforcement helps to build self-esteem and respect. When you catch students doing what you want them to do it is important to recognize them and consistently praise each specific incident.

⇒ "Thank you Sally for raising your hand and waiting to be called on."

⇒ "Joseph, I like the way that you are sitting quietly and waiting for instructions."

⇒ "I like the way that the blue group is using their "six-inch" voices while they are talking."

⇒ "First graders, it makes me so happy when you are all settled down and waiting to begin our lesson! Thank you!"

Examples of positive reinforcement in the classroom

1. Acknowledging students' appropriate behavior and praising them for it is a great way to be proactive.
This should occur in all settings and at all times.

2. Reward students with classroom jobs and responsibilities.

3. Try not to use major incentives and rewards unless necessary.
Start with easy, small rewards and incentives.

4. Allow students to work for tangible or edible rewards (stickers, prizes, food).

5. Try these ideas to use as a reinforcer
* Playing a game with a friend
* Earning "free time"
* Eating breakfast or lunch with the teacher
* Reading or looking at magazines
* Using the computer alone or with a friend
* Listening to music with a tape recorder and earphones
* Working with clay, special pens/paper, whiteboards
* Skipping an assignments of student's choice

b. Classroom Incentives

Classroom incentives are motivators to use for entire classes. (These two suggested incentives can be adapted in any way to meet the needs of any classroom.)

1. Students earn tickets or play money.
These tickets or play money are used towards a weekly, biweekly, or monthly auction or raffle. Students can use their accumulated tickets/money/points to buy assorted toys, items, or privileges from their teacher.

2. Marbles, beans, or chips in a jar.
When students are caught doing something well or behaving appropriately the teacher will put a marble, bean or chip in a jar. When the jar is full, the class earns a special party (popcorn, pizza, ice cream), activity (video), or field trip. Students should know what the party, activity or field trip will be, so students know what they will be working toward.

c. Assertive Discipline

Students must know what will happen when they are both following and not following the rules. One use of consequences is to use warnings with incremental consequences when students do not follow the rules. When students are following the rules, you should give positive attention. Students must know from the beginning what the consequences will be for not following the rules. Various classroom management systems include the following:

1. Color Coded Cards.
This is a system for monitoring behavior of the entire classroom. There are many variations of this system, thus it can be changed to meet the different needs of the different classrooms. It may involve using a pocket chart with an individual envelope or compartment for each student, identified by that student's name. All students start the day with a green card in the envelopes meaning every one is ready to GO. When there is a rule infraction, after a WARNING, the color of the individual's card is changed to yellow. This is a warning, indicating that the student must watch what is happening and needs to slow down. With the next rule infraction, the card is changed to the final card which is red or STOP. This

results in a severe consequence, such as loss of recess, time away from the class, or a call to a parent. These consequences will be set up and clearly explained to all students prior to initiating this system.

With this system, students start each day with a clean slate. For some classes, especially younger ones, it may be wise to start each morning and afternoon with a clean slate. For greatest effectiveness, allow your class to define the consequences associated with the change of each colored card. If you don't want the chart posted for all to see, it is also possible that each student starts the day with a green card at his or her desk. If the card is needing to be changed, the teacher can individually and privately go to the student's desk and change the card quietly, with few others noticing.

Another variation of this system is to link each classroom rule to a certain color. When a student breaks a specific rule, the teacher places that color card corresponding to the rule broken into the student's pocket. This way, students are clearly aware of the rule that they did not follow. The same progressive consequences which were explained above also follow the change of each card.

2. Numbered Cards.

If a parent-teacher communication monitoring system would be effective, a behavioral monitoring system is one that would go home each day with the students. Each student would receive a numbered card, indicating the type of day that was had at school.

> 5 - Very well behaved. Great day!
> 4 - Good day.
> 3 - So-so day.
> 2 - We had some trouble today
> 1 - We had a very difficult day today

Many teachers like to set up a parent/school communication system where parents are informed of the type of day or week that their child had by sending home a number. Prior to starting this system, parents are informed of what each number means. Teachers will send home a daily/weekly notice with the number written on it. Students are then responsible to make sure their parent(s) sees the notice and then signs it. The student must also be sure to return the notice back to school the next school day.

Obviously, not all students will need this type of behavior monitoring, but it has been known to work very well for those who need it and for those who have parents who will support it.

3. Token Economy/ Response Costs.

Some teachers use a system of rewards and then fines (response cost). For example, using plastic colored links, you could assign a monetary or number value to four colors of the links: yellow = penny or 1 point, red = nickel or 2 points, green = dime or 3 points, and blue = quarter or 4 points. The teacher "pays" the students for good behavior by receiving a certain color link. Specific behaviors would be attached to the different point or monetary values. This is the positive reinforcement "token economy" part of the system. When there are rule infractions, the teacher "fines" the whole calss for the specific offense. This is the "response cost" part of the system. These specific fines will be set up prior to initiating this system as well. It is important to try and discuss a variety of rule infractions that are possible. Every week (Friday's are often good day for this), students are allowed to shop at the classroom store with the points or money that they have earned.

This system can work for the whole class or on an individual basis. The whole class can earn points and the teacher awards all students a certain value for their links; or individuals can earn points for on-task behavior, or whatever specific behaviors are being targeted for that student.

This token economy/response cost system can be adapted and adjusted to meet the needs of any teacher in any classroom. It is quite effective and not very difficult to manage. Examples of "treats" to have available for students to buy could include: a. Pencils b. Pens c. Paper d. Crayons e. Candies
Students love just about anything; however, it is essential to keep the "treats" of interest to the students so they feel the need to keep working toward those prizes.

d. Time outs and Time aways

Time outs and time aways are good ways to allow students to calm down and help regain control if the stimulation in the classroom is causing the student to become worked up or out of control. Use time outs and time aways as needed to be effective in your classroom. It is important not to view time outs as negative and intrusive. They can be very effective and unintrusive when handled appropriately.

1. Remain in the classroom, but away from distractions.
A corner of the room or sitting in a bean bag chair, or in an empty desk, away from the other student desks.

2. Partner up with another teacher (preferably from a different grade)
For time outs. If a student needs a time away, the students can go to the receiving classroom with an independent assignment to work on for a specified amount of time.

3. Allow the student to go to the counselor's office for a few minutes.

Tips for time outs and time aways

* **Remain calm and positive while you are directing the student to time out**. For example: "Jesse, I would like for you to sit quietly and without making noises. If you can't do that, then go back to your desk. You can join our activity again when you feel you will be able to sit quietly with the rest of the class."

❋ **Try a "think-about-it" chair for a specified amount of time**. Instruct them to think about their inappropriate behavior and what they would do differently. A good rule of thumb is about one minute of time per year of age. A six-year-old may have about a six minute time out.

❋ **After a time away, if the student continues the behavior,** he or she should   to be sent out of the room or to the counseling center to avoid inappropriate negative attention from the rest of the class.

❋ **It is often very effective to call home or to the parent's workplace** together with the student, if a student's behavior is becoming disruptive to the rest of the class.

❋ **Be sure not to overuse time outs** and be sure that the student is always aware of the behavior that caused him or her to receive the time out.

e. Behavior Contracts

Behavior contracts are an agreement made between the student and the teacher. A contract must specifically state what behavior is expected and what the reinforcement or reward will be when the behavior/task is completed. Behavior contracts are effective with students. The effectiveness, however, can be short-lived and the rewards/systems may need to be changed frequently. Parental involvement and support is imperative. (See example behavioral contracts on pages 100 and 101)

f. Proximity Control

While circulating in the classroom, try to be near the students with the attention and behavioral problems. Sometimes a hand on the shoulder or eye contact with a quick reminder is effective. It is often effective to place children with behavioral or attention difficulties to sit next to the teacher or next to or between well-focused students. Avoid seating these students near learning centers, the door, windows, or other distracters. Proximity control seems quite simple, but does have a very good effect on students who need constant reminders to return to task.

g. Preventative Cueing

This is a technique for catching the disruptive behavior before they begin and also for avoiding confrontation or embarrassment of the student in front of peers. Before beginning this technique, arrange privately with the student a specific hand signal or word signal to use that will remind the student to calm down, pay attention, stop talking out, or whatever other behavior the student is struggling with. Here are some examples of some cueing reminders.

1. Use a traffic light or stop sign signal.

This will help to remind students to slow down or stop the behavior their behavior.

2. Get eye contact with the student and point to your eyes

This would help to indicate that you want him or her to focus on you.

3. Use the "thumbs up" sign.

You could use this sign, or any other that is agreed upon between you and the student. When the student sees that you are using this sign, this will tell him or her that he or she can get up and move to another part of the room, in order to aid in concentration.

h. Self- Monitoring

Self-monitoring is one of the least intrusive and least restrictive methods of monitoring one's behavior. With self-monitoring, a target behavior for the student is chosen for the student to record. An example would be thumb-sucking. Every time the teacher or the student "catches" the student sucking his or her thumb, the student would make a recording (a tally mark on a slip of paper.) At the end of the day, the tally marks would be totaled. The teacher and student should have a pre-set reward/response cost system set up. If the student reaches the goal set, the reward will be given. If the student does not reach that goal for the day, the response cost is issued. Recording one's own behavior is an effective way to increase behaviors such as academic productivity and on task behavior, or decrease inappropriate behaviors such as thumb sucking, talking out, or making inappropriate noises.

i. Planned Ignoring

Planned ignoring is a way to decrease those inappropriate, attention-seeking behaviors. This means that the teacher purposefully ignores the behavior, because the student is exhibiting the behavior in order to receive the teacher's attention. Obviously, the behavior can only be ignored if it is one that is not destructive to the student or others. When attempting this strategy, teachers should be aware that the behavior will most likely **increase** for the first little bit, as the student will be "testing" the teacher to see if he or she can "make" the teacher pay attention to him or her. Hang in there! It will get better! Be strong. If the behavior is impacting the education of the other students and it is not seeming to get any better, stop this strategy and attempt another one.

Contract

I _____

agree to: _____

_____

_____

_____

My hard work will earn: _____

_____

_____

_____

We will meet again to discuss this contract on:

_____

_____   _____
Student's Signature   Date

_____   _____
Teacher's Signature   Date

Contract

I agree to:

On or before _____

day or date

Signed _____

Student's signature

My work will earn:

Signed _____

Teacher's signature

Date _____

III. How do I do handle this behavior?

Here are some strategies to try with students who are exhibiting behaviors in the classroom that are interfering with your guidelines and expectations or with other students ability to learn and you would like to have the frequency of those behaviors **decrease**, or the behaviors are very appropriate but are not occurring as frequently as you would so you want those behavior to **increase**. I have taken specific behaviors that seem to be mentioned most often by teachers. The suggestions are given with the least restrictive, least intrusive interventions first, leading up to the more restrictive interventions. It is my suggestion to attempt the least intrusive first before trying the more intrusive. All suggestions given can and should be modified or changed to better meet the needs in your classroom when necessary.

Behaviors to decrease:
1) **Out of seat**
2) **Blurting out**
3) **Inappropriate noises**
4) **Intentionally falling out of seat**
5) **Interrupting the teacher**
6) **Being off-task**

Behaviors to increase:
7) **Assignment Completion**
8) **Following directions on the 1st request given**

1. Out of Seat

How can I effectively help the student who is constantly out of his or her seat?

1. Proximity Control.

Place the student's desk next to your desk. Being physically close by this student may help to remind the student to remain in his or her seat, if you are sitting near.

2. Positive Reinforcement.

Praise the student, privately if the student is easily embarrassed by attention, for remaining in his or her seat. "Wow, Johnny, I haven't seen you get out of your seat for 10 minutes. You are really working hard. Good for you! Keep it up!"

3. Self-monitor/preventative cueing.

Have a premade form or chart on or inside the student's desk. Anytime the student is out of seat, give the student some sort of cue (pointing the index finger at his or her desk) to tell the student to go back and make a tally mark on his or her form. The student may also start "catching" him or herself out of his or her seat and will make tally marks on his or her own. At the beginning of the week or day, have a predetermined number that you want that student to be under by the end of the day. This number will be determined depending on how often the student is normally out of his or her seat. If the student is out of his or her seat an average of 10 times per day, the first day you start this system the goal for the student may be to only be out of his or her seat 9 times that day. Start small; that way, you are more likely to see results quickly. Prior to starting the system, a reward system should be put into place, therefore, if the student meets the goal for the day or week, he or she will earn the reward for that day. If the student does not meet the goal, the student does not receive the reward for that day or week.

4. Token economy/response cost.

The student starts the day with a certain number of "points". Every time the student is out of seat, a point gets taken away. For example if a student starts with 10 points and is out of seat five times during the day, he or she will have 5 points left at the end of the day. The student and you should determine how many points a student needs to have at the end of the day (or week) in order to earn or buy a privilege or treat. If the student does not have enough points, the response cost is that he or she will not have any points to "spend." Be sure that the goal is attainable, yet not too easy.

2. Talking or Blurting Out

How do I effectively help the student who is always talking without permission or blurting out in the middle of a lesson?

1. Proximity Control.

Place the student's desk next to your desk. This may be all that is necessary to remind a student to raise his or her hand before talking or to stop him or herself before talking out. Even a touch on the shoulder may remind a student to stop talking.

2. Positive Reinforcement.

Praise the student, privately if the student is easily embarrassed by attention, for not talking out. "Wow, Johnny, I haven't heard you blurt out all morning. You are really working hard. Good for you! Keep it up!"

3. Planned Ignoring.

Often times a student will talk out to get attention, even if the attention is negative. Your reprimanding the student for talking out may still be reinforcing to the student. Therefore, ignoring the student who is talking out, by not giving him or her any response to the behavior, will show the student that he or she will not get your attention by talking out. Keep in mind that the behavior may increase for a period of time, as the student may feel as though he or she has to try even harder for your attention. You need to be patient and allow for this. Eventually, the student will realize that you are not going to provide the attention he or she is looking for. If the talking out behavior becomes too intrusive for the rest of the class and is interfering with the class's ability to learn, another strategy should be tried.

4. Self-Monitor.

Have a premade form or chart on or inside the student's desk. Anytime the student is talking or blurting out, give the student some sort of cue (getting eye contact and touching your nose) to tell the student to make a tally mark on his or her chart. The student may also start "catching" him or herself talking or blurting out and will make marks on his or her own. This is the ultimate goal of the strategy! At the beginning of the day or week, have a predetermined goal or number of tally marks that you want the student to be under for the day or week. This number will be determined depending on how often the student normally blurts out during the day. If the student talks or blurts out an average of 10 times per day, the first day you start this system the goal for the student may be to blurt out only 9 times that day. Start small; that way, you are more likely to see results quickly. If the student meets the goal for the day or week, he/she will receive a reward from a pre-set reward system. If the student does not meet the goal, the student will not receive the reward.

5. Token Economy/Response Cost.

The student starts the day with a certain number of "points". Every time the student talks or blurts out, a point gets taken away. For example if a student starts with 10 points and blurts out 5 times during the day, he or she will have 5 points left at the end of the day. The student and you should determine how many points he or she needs to have at the end of the day (or week) in order to earn or buy a privilege or treat. If the student does not have enough points, the response cost is that he or she will not have any points to "spend."If the student loses all points during the day, an additional negative consequence should follow, such as a time away, or an additional loss of privilege. The key is to make sure the goal of number of points is attainable, yet not too easy.

6. Behavior Contract.

Write a contract with the student that states that he or she will raise his or her hand and wait to be called upon before talking out during class. Positive reinforcements and rewards should be put into place when requirements listed on the contract are met. Consequences will follow if requirements are not met. The importance of a contract is to involve the student completely and have the student and you sign the contract. The student should have a copy of the contract to serve as a visual reminder at all times. (See example behavior contracts on pages 100 and 101)

3. Making inappropriate noises

How do I help the student who is constantly making inappropriate noises and being disruptive in my classroom?

1. Proximity Control.

Place the student's desk next to your desk. This may be all that is necessary to remind a student to refrain from making inappropriate noises. Even a touch on the shoulder may remind a student to stop making noise.

2. Positive Reinforcement.

Praise the student, privately if the student is easily embarrassed by attention, for remaining in seat. "Wow, Johnny, I haven't heard you make any noises for 10 minutes. You are really working hard. Good for you! Keep it up!"

3. Planned Ignoring.

Often times a student will make noises to get attention even if the attention is negative. Therefore, ignoring the student who is making noises, by not giving him or her any response to the behavior, will show the student that he or she will not get attention by making noise. Keep in mind that the behavior may increase for a period of time, as the student may feel like he or she has to try even harder for your attention. Be patient and allow for the increase and eventually, the student will realize that you are not going to provide the attention he or she is looking or. If the noise-making behavior becomes too intrusive for the rest of the class and is interfering with the class's ability to learn, another strategy should be tried.

4. Self-Monitor.

Have a premade form or chart on or inside the student's desk. Anytime the student is making noises, give the student some sort of cue (getting eye contact and touching your nose) to tell the student to make a mark on his or her form. The student may also start "catching" him or herself making noises and will make marks on his or her own. This is the ultimate goal of the strategy!

At the beginning of the week or day, have a predetermined number of marks that you want that student to be under by the end of the day or week. This number will be determined depending on how often the student normally makes noise during an average day. If the student makes noises on an average of 10 times per day, the first day you start this system the goal for the student may be to make noise only 9 times that day. Start small; that way, you are more likely to see results quickly. If the student meets the goal for the day or week, he or she will receive a reward from a pre-set reward system. If the student does not meet the goal, the student does not receive the reward.

5. Token Economy/Response Cost.

The student starts the day with a certain number of chips in a cup. Every time the student is heard making noises, take a chip out of the cup. For example if a student starts with 10 chips in the cup and is heard making noise 5 times during the day, he or she will have 5 chips left in the cup at the end of the day. The student and you should determine how many chips he or she needs to have at the end of the day in order to earn or buy a privilege or treat. If the student does not have enough chips in the cup, the response cost is that he or she will not have any points to "spend." If the student loses all chips during the day, an additional negative consequence should follow, such as a time away, or an additional loss of privilege. The key is to make sure the goal at the end of the day is attainable, yet not too easy.

6. Behavior Contract.

Write a contract with the student that states that he or she will remain quiet and refrain from making noise in class. Positive reinforcements should be put into place when requirements listed on the contract are met. Consequences will be provided if requirements are not met. The importance of a contract is to involve the student completely and have the student and you sign and date the contract. The student should have a copy of the contract to be a visual reminder at all times. (See example contracts on pages 100 and 101)

4. Falling out of seat

How do I help the student who is continually falling out of his or her seat (or any other attention seeking behavior) in an attempt to receive attention from me or the peers in the classroom?

1. Proximity Control.

Place the student's desk next to your desk. This may be all that is necessary to remind a student to remain in his or her seat.

2. Positive Reinforcement.

Praise the student, privately if the student is easily embarrassed by attention, for remaining in seat. "Wow, Johnny, I haven't seen you fall out of your seat for 10 minutes. You are really working hard. Good for you! Keep it up!"

3. Planned Ignoring.

Often times a student will fall out of his or her seat (or try other behaviors) in order to get attention from the teacher or other classmates. even if the attention is negative. Therefore, ignoring the student who is falling out of his of her seat, by not giving him or her any response to the behavior, will show the student that he or she will not get attention by falling out of his or her seat. (Discuss with the rest of the class the importance of ignoring inappropriate behaviors that are occurring around the classroom, so that the student is not being reinforced by his or her peers as well.) Keep in mind that the behavior may increase for a period of time, as the student may feel like he or she has to try even harder for your attention. Be patient and allow for the increase and eventually, the student will realize that you are not going to provide the attention he or she is looking for. Of course if the behavior becomes too intrusive for the rest of the class, try a different strategy.

4. Self-Monitor.

Have a premade form or chart on or inside the student's desk. Anytime the student falls out of his or her desk, (or exhibits any other "attention seeking" type behavior), give the student some sort of cue (getting eye contact and touching your nose) to tell the student to make a tally mark on his or her form. The student may also start "catching" him or herself falling exhibiting the attention seeking behaviors and will make marks on his or her own. This is the ultimate goal of the strategy!

At the beginning of the week or day, have a predetermined number or tally marks that you want that student to be under by the end of the day or week. This number will be determined depending on how often the student normally falls out of the desk (or any other attention seeking behavior) during the day. If the student falls out of the desk an average of 10 times per day, the first day you start this system the goal for the student may be to fall out only 9 times that day. Start small; that way, you are more likely to see results quickly. If the student meets the goal for the day, he or she will receive an award from a pre-set reward system. If the student does not meet the goal, the student does not receive the reward.

5. Token Economy/Response Cost.

The student starts the day with a certain number of chips in a cup. Every time the student falls out of the desk, take a chip out of the cup. For example if a student starts with 10 chips in the cup and falls out of the desk 5 times during the day, he or she will have 5 chips left in the cup at the end of the day. The student and you should determine how many chips a student needs to have at the end of the day in order to earn or buy a privilege or treat. If the student does not have enough chips in the cup, the response cost is that he or she will not have any points to "spend." If the student loses all chips during the day, an additional negative consequence should follow, such as a time away, or an additional loss of privilege. The key is to make sure the goal at the end of the day is attainable, yet not too easy.

6. Behavior Contract.

Write a contract, with the student, that states that he or she will remain in his or her desk (or whatever the attention-seeking behavior is), only falling out a certain number of times. Positive reinforcements should be put into place when requirements listed on the contract are met. Consequences will be provided if requirements are not met. The importance of a contract is to involve the student completely and have the student and you sign and date the contract. The student should have a copy of the contract to serve as a visual reminder at all times. (See example contracts on pages 100 and 101)

5. Interrupting the Teacher

How do I help the student who is continually interrupting me, classmates, or other adults in my classroom?

1. Positive Reinforcement:

Praise the student, privately if the student is easily embarrassed by attention, for remaining in seat. "Wow, Johnny, you are really working hard. I haven't had to remind you to not interrupt. Good for you! Keep it up!"

2. Planned Ignoring.

Often times a student will interrupt the teacher or others in order to get attention, even if the attention is negative. Ignoring the student who is interrupting you, by not giving him or her any response to the behavior, and not answering the student's question or comment, will show the student that he or she will not get attention by interrupting. Keep in mind that the behavior may increase for a period of time, as the student may feel like he or she has to try even harder for your attention. Be patient and allow for the increase and eventually, the student will realize that you are not going to provide the attention he or she is looking for.

4. Self-Monitor.

Have a pre-made form or chart on or inside the student's desk. Anytime the student interrupts, give the student some sort of cue (getting eye contact and touching your nose) to tell the student to make a mark on his or her chart. The student may also start "catching" him or herself interrupting and will make marks on his or her own. This is the ultimate goal of the strategy!

At the beginning of the week or day, have a predetermined number of tally marks that you want that student to be under by the end of that day or week. This number will be determined depending on how often the student normally interrupts during the day. If the student interrupts on the average of 10 times per day, the first day you start this system the goal for the student may be to interrupt only 9 times that day. Start small; that way, you are more likely to see results quickly. If the student meets the goal for the day, he or she will receive a reinforcement from a pre-set reward system. If the student does not meet the goal, the student will not receive the reward.

5. Token Economy/Response Cost.

The student starts the day with a certain number of points. Every time the student interrupts, take a point away. For example if a student starts with 10 points and interrupts you 5 times during the day, he or she will have 5 points left at the end of the day. The student and you should determine how many points a student needs to have at the end of the day in order to earn or buy a privilege or treat. If the student does not have enough points, the response cost is that he or she will not have any points to "spend." If the student loses all points during the day, an additional negative consequence should follow, such as a time away, or an additional loss of privilege. The key is to make sure the goal is attainable, yet not too easy.

6. Behavior Contract.

Write a contract with the student that states that he or she will not interrupt the teacher or any others. Positive reinforcements should be put into place when requirements listed on the contract are met. Consequences will be provided if requirements are not met. The importance of a contract is to involve the student completely and have the student and you sign and date the contract. The student should have a copy of the contract to be a visual reminder at all times. (See example contracts on pages 100 and 101)

6. Off task behavior

How do I help with the child who is always off-task and not paying attention to what is asked of him or her?

1. Positive Reinforcement.

Praise the student, privately if the student is easily embarrassed by attention, for remaining on task. "Wow, Johnny, you are really working hard. You have been on-task for 10 minutes. Good for you! Keep it up!"

2. Self-Monitor.

Have a premade form or chart on or inside the student's desk. Anytime the student is off-task, give the student some sort of cue (getting eye contact and touching your nose) to tell the student to make a tally mark on his or her form. The student may also start "catching" him or herself off-task and will make the tally marks on his or her own. This is the ultimate goal of the strategy! At the beginning of the day or week, have a predetermined number of tally marks that you want that student to be under by the end of the day or week. This number will be determined depending on how often the student is normally off-task during the day. If the student is off-task on the average of 10 times per day, the first day you start this system, the goal for the student may be to be off-task only 9 times that day. Start small; that way, you are more likely to see results quickly. If the student meets the goal for the day, he or she will receive a positive reinforcement from a pre-set reward system. If the student does not meet the goal, the student does not receive the reward.

3. Token Economy/Response Cost.

The student starts the day with a certain number of points. Every time the student is off-task, take a point away. For example if a student starts with 10 points and is found to be off-task 5 times during the day, he or she will have 5 points left at the end of the day. The student and you should determine how many points he or she needs to have at the end of the day in order to earn or buy a privilege or treat. If the student does not have enough points, the response cost is that he or she will not have any points to "spend." If the student loses all points during the day, an additional negative consequence should follow, such as a time away, or an additional loss of privilege. The key is to make sure the goal is attainable, yet not too easy.

4. Behavior Contract.

Write a contract with the student that states that he or she will remain on-task during the day and will only be reminded to return to task a certain number each day. Positive reinforcements should be put into place when requirements listed on the contract are met. Consequences will follow if requirements are not met. The importance of a contract is to involve the student completely and have the student and you sign and date the contract. The student should have a copy of the contract to serve as a visual reminder at all times. (See example contracts on pages 100 and 101)

7. Completing assignments

How do I help the student who is unable to or refuses to complete his or her assignments?

1. Positive Reinforcement.

Praise the student, privately if the student is easily embarrassed by attention, for completing his or her assignments. "Wow, Johnny, you have completed all of your assignments today. You are really working hard. Good for you! Keep it up!"

2. Self-Monitor.

Have a premade form or chart on or inside the student's desk. Everytime the student completes an assignment, he or she can make a tally mark on his or her form. The ultimate goal of the strategy is to get the student to make the tally marks without reminders after every completed assignment!

At the beginning of the week or day, have a predetermined % of assignments that you want that student to complete each day or week. This number will be determined depending on the % of assignments the student normally completes. If the student completes an average of 50% of his or her assignments, the first day you start this system the goal for the student may be to complete 55% of the assignments for the day. Start small; that way, you are more likely to see results quickly. If the student meets the goal for the day, he or she will receive a positive reinforcement from a pre-set reward system. If the student does not meet the goal, the student does not receive the reward. As the behavior begins to increase, increase the goal.

3. Token Economy/Response Cost.

The student starts the day with an empty cup. Everytime the student completes an assignment, he or she can place a chip in that cup. At the end of the day, count the chips and see if the student has matched or exceeded the predetermined number of chips necessary for the reward. If the student has enough chips, he or she may earn a privilege or treat. If he or she has not met the specified number of chips, he or she does not earn the reward.

4. Behavior Contract.

Write a contract, with the student, that states that he or she will complete a certain % of assignments every day. Positive reinforcements should be put into place when requirements listed on the contract are met. Consequences will be provided if requirements are not met. The importance of a contract is to involve the student completely and have the student and you sign and date the contract. The student should have a copy of the contract to serve as as visual reminder at all times. (See example contracts on pages 100 and 101)

8. Follow directions on the 1ˢᵗ request given

How do I help the child who refuses to follow directions on the 1st request given?

1. Positive Reinforcement.

Praise the student, privately if the student is easily embarrassed by attention, for following direction on the 1st request. "Wow, Johnny, you followed my directions the 1st time I asked, you are really working hard, good for you! Keep it up!"

2. Self-Monitor.

Have a premade form on or inside the student's desk. Everytime the student follows directions on the 1st request, he or she can make a tally mark on the form. The ultimate goal of the strategy is to get the student to recognize that he or she is following directions and will make the tally marks independently. At the beginning of the week or day, have a predetermined number of tally marks that you want that student to have at the end of each day or week. This number will be determined depending on the number of times the student normally follows direction on the initial request. If the student only follows initial direction 2 times each day, the first day you start this system, the goal for the student may be to follow direction on the initial request 3 times for the day. Start small, that way, you are more likely to see results quickly. If the student meets the goal for the day, he or she will receive a positive reinforcer from a pre-set reward system. If the student does not meet the goal, the student does not receive the reward. As the behavior begins to increase, increase the goal.

3. Token Economy/Response Cost.

The student starts the day with an empty cup. Everytime the student follows directions on the first request, he or she can place a chip in that cup. At the end of the day, count the chips and see if the student has matched or exceeded the predetermined number of chips necessary for the reward. If the student has enough chips, he or she may earn a privilege or treat. If he or she has not met the specified number of chips, he or she does not earn the reward.

4. Behavior Contract.

Write a contract with the student that states that he or she will follow directions on the first request a certain number of times each day. Positive reinforcements should be put into place when requirements listed on the contract are met. Consequences will be provided if requirements are not met. The importance of a contract is to involve the student completely and have the student and you sign and date the contract. The student should have a copy of the contract to serve as a visual reminder at all times. (See example contracts on pages 100 and 101).

Section IV

Medications

Medications

> **Disclaimer** - The information presented in this section on medications was taken directly from informational handouts provided for use in the resource book *Helping Parents, Youth, and Teachers Understand Medications for Behavioral and Emotional Problems: A Resource Book of Medication Information Handouts.* (See the reference section on page 184 for a complete reference citation.) This section is intended as a general reference **ONLY** and is not intended to replace the opinion and/or advise of medical personal

To help many children show and feel success in school, doctors are prescribing medication to combat some of the interfering factors. Children are being medicated for many different reasons including to assist with ADD/ADHD, anxiety, depression, emotional and behavioral problems, allergies, and seizures or convulsions. Listed and described below are **some** of the common medications that are being prescribed to school age children. A description of the medication is given as well as side effects that may be noticed from these medications.

General information about medication

Each child and adolescent is different and not one child or person has exactly the same combination of medical and psychological problems. When you are working with a child who is prescribed medication, it is a good idea to talk with the parents with regards to the reasons that this child is medicated. If the parents give permission, it would also be helpful and useful to talk with the doctor responsible for prescribing the medicine. It is important to administer the medication exactly as the doctor instructs. If a doseage of medication is forgotten while a child is in school, there may be special circumstances which will need to be followed. It is a good idea to ask the parents in advance what should occur if this were to happen. A school is not allowed, without parental permission, to stop or change the ways of administering the medication. Many times, a medication is required to be taken with food, but lunchtime or snack time may change. If this is the case be sure to notify the parent so that appropriate adjustments can be made.

If it appears to you, by the child's behavior in your classroom, that a medication is no longer being positiviely affective, this could mean that it is not being taken regularly. The student may be "cheeking" or hiding the medicine or forgetting to take it. Please inform the child's parents if you are noticing changes. Taking medication is a private matter and must be handled discreetly and confidentially. It is important to be sensitive to the students' feelings about taking the medicine.

Each medicine has a "generic" or chemical name. Just like laundry soap or paper towels, some medicines are sold by more than one company under different brand names. The same medicine may be available under a generic name and several brand names. It is important to know if the medication is a generic name or a brand name.

1.- Anticonvulsants

What are Anticonvulsants?

Anticonvulsants are usually used to treat seizures (convulsions). They are **sometimes** used to treat behavioral problems even if the student does not have seizures.

How can these medicines help?

Anticonvulsant medications can control seizure activity as well as reduce aggression, anger, and severe mood swings.

What are the common anticonvulstants used?

Brand Name	Generic Name
Tegretol	carbamazepine
Depakene or Depakote	valproate or valproic acid
Klonopin	clonazepam

How do these medicines work?

Anticonvulsants are thought to work by stabilizing a part of the brain cell or by increasing the concentration of certain chemicals in the brain.

What side effects might be seen from these medicines?

Any medication can have side effects, including an allergy to the medicine itself. Notify the student's parents and school nurse immediately if any of the following side effects appear or if you think that the medicine is causing any other problems.

Tegretol (Carbamazepine)

Common side effects, especially at first
* Double or blurred vision
* Sleepiness
* Dizziness
* Clumsiness or decreased coordination

* Mild nausea or upset stomach
* Hair loss
* Increase risk of sunburn
* Skin rash (may indicate allergic reaction)

Behavioral and emotional side effects
* Anxiety or nervousness
* Agitation or mania
* Impulsive or irritable behavior
* Motor or vocal tics (Fast, repeated sounds)
* Increased aggression
* Hallucinations

Serious, but very rare, side effects

* Severe behavior problems
* Severe skin rash
* Worsening of seizures

* Loss of appetite
* Yellowing of skin or eyes
* Swelling of legs or feet

* Lung irritation
* Vomiting
* Unusual bruising or bleeding

Depakene/Depakote (Valproic Acid)

Common side effects, especially at first	Behavioral and emotional side effects
❋ Upset stomach	❋ Increased aggression
❋ Increased appetite	❋ Increased irritability
❋ Thinning hair	
❋ Tremors (shakiness)	
❋ Drowsiness	
❋ Weight gain	

Serious, but very rare, side effects

❋ Feeling sick or unusually tired for no reason	❋ Loss of appetite
❋ Yellowing of skin or eyes	❋ Swelling of legs or feet
❋ Unusual bruising or bleeding	❋ Sore throat or fever
❋ Mouth ulcers	❋ Vomiting
❋ Skin rash	❋ Severe behavior problems

Klonopin (Clonazepam)

Common side effects, especially at first	Behavioral and emotional side effects
❋ Difficulty with balance	❋ Irritability
❋ Drowsiness/ sleepiness	❋ Excitement
	❋ Increased anger/aggression
	❋ Trouble sleeping or nightmares
	❋ Memory loss

Serious, but very rare, side effects

❋ Uncontrollable behavior	❋ If combined with alcohol - severe sleepiness, unconsciousness, DEATH

What could happen if these medicines are stopped suddenly?

If carbamazepine or valproic acid is stopped suddenly, uncomfortable withdrawal symptoms will occur. If clonazepam is stopped suddenly, seizures could result if the child is being treated for seizures.

How long will these medicines be needed?

The length of time a person needs to take an Anticonvulsant depends on what disorder is being treated. For example with an impulse-control disorder, a person usually takes an Anticonvulsant only until behavior therapy begins to work. Someone with bipolar disorder may need to take Anticonvulsants for many years.

2.- Antihistamines

What are Antihistamines?

Antihistamines were developed to treat allergies. They are often used in children. They may be used to treat **anxiety, insomnia, or side effects** of certain other medicines.

How can these medicines help?

Antihistamines may decrease nervousness. They work best for anxiety when used for a short time along with therapy. Occasionally they are used for longer periods of time to treat anxiety that remains after therapy is completed. They can also be used to help with insomnia when used for a short time along with a behavioral program.

What are the common antihistamines used?

Brand Name	Generic Name
Benedryl	diphenhydramine
Atarax or Vistaril	hydroxyzine
Periactin	cyproheptadine

How do these medicines work?

Antihistamines help reduce anxiety because of their sedation side effect. They make people a little sleepy so that they feel less nervous and tense.

What side effects might be seen from these medicines?

The most common side effect is sleepiness. If the medicine is causing drowsiness, it is very important that the child or adolescent to not drive a car, ride a bicycle or motorcycle, or operate machinery. Decreased attention or learning will usually be obvious.

Common side effects of Antihistamines

* ⁕ Sleepiness
* ⁕ Decreased attention of learning in school
* ⁕ Dry mouth (allow students to take drinks)
* ⁕ Blurred vision (trouble seeing blackboard)
* ⁕ Constipation (allow student to drink more)
* ⁕ Dizziness (when stands up quickly)
* ⁕ Loss of appetite, nausea, or upset stomach

Less common side effects

* ⁕ Poor coordination
* ⁕ Motor tics (fast repeated movements)
* ⁕ Unusual muscle movement
* ⁕ Irritability, overactivity

Serious, but rare side effects
- ❋ Worsening of asthma
- ❋ Seizures, muscle stiffness
- ❋ Uncontrollable behavior

What could happen if these medicines are stopped suddenly?

Stopping these medicines suddenly does not usually cause problems. Diarrhea or feeling ill may result.

How long will these medicines be needed?

Antihistamines are usually prescribed for only a few weeks to allow the patient to be calm enough to learn new ways to cope with anxiety.

3.- Antianxiety Medication

What are Antianxiety medications?

Several groups of medicines, often called sedatives or tranquilizers, are used to treat anxiety. The medicines most often used to treat anxiety or sleep problems are placed in two general groups - benzodiazepines and nonbenzodiazepines. The nonbenzodiazapines include BuSpar, Antihistamines, and Beta-Blockers, which are covered on upcoming pages.

Benzodiazepines

How can these medicines help?

Antianxiety medicines decrease nervousness, fears, and excessive worrying. The benzodiazepines are particularly effective in decreasing the severe physical symptoms of anxiety disorders such as panic attacks and phobias. These medications are used for a short time when symptoms are very uncomfortable or frightening and make it difficult to do important things such as go to school.

Benzodiazepines can also be used for sleep problems, such as night terrors or sleepwalking, that are dangerous or are making it impossible for other family members to get enough sleep

What are the common Antianxiety medications: Benzodiazepines used?

Usually used to decrease anxiety, panic or night terrors

Brand Name	Generic Name
Ativan	lorazepam
Klonopin	clonazepam
Librium	chlordiazepoxide
Valium	diazepam
Xanax	alprazolam

Usually used to treat sleep problems

Dalmane	flurazepam

How do these medicines work?

Antianxiety medicines work by calming the parts of the brain that are too excitable in anxious people. For example, they can help anxious people to be calm enough to learn, and with therapy, to understand and tolerate their worries or fears and even to overcome them.

What side effects might be seen from these medications?

The most common side effect is sleepiness. If the medicine is causing drowsiness, it is very important that the child or adolescent does not drive a car, ride a bicycle or motorcycle, or operate machinery. Benzodiazepines must not be combined with alcohol: severe sleepiness, or even unconsciousness, may result.

These medicines are usually safe when used for short periods of time as the doctor prescribes. Becoming dependent and addicted to benzodiazepines is possible, but that is not a great problem for patients who see their doctor regularly.

Sometimes antianxiety medicines seem to work backward, causing excitement, irritability, anger, aggression, trouble sleeping, nightmares, uncontrollable behavior, or memory loss. Call parents right away if you see this happening.

What could happen if these medicines are stopped suddenly?

Many medicines cause problems if stopped suddenly. Problems are more likely to occur in patients taking high doses of benzodiazepines for 2 months or longer, but it is important to stop the medicine slowly even after a few weeks. Common withdrawal symptoms may include anxiety, irritability, shaking, sweating, aches and pains, muscle cramps, vomiting and trouble sleeping. If large doses are stopped suddenly, seizures, hallucinations, or out-of-control behavior may result.

How long will these medicines be needed?

Benzodiazepines are usually prescribed for only a few weeks to allow the patient to be calm enough to learn new ways to cope with anxiety and to allow the nervous system to reset to a less excitable state. Each person is unique and some may need the medicines for months or years.

Buspar

How can this medicine help?

Antianxiety medicines decrease nervousness, fears, and excessive worrying. These drugs are used for a short time when symptoms are very uncomfortable or frightening, or when they make it hard to do important things such as go to school. Occasionally they are used for longer periods to treat anxiety that remains after therapy is completed. BuSpar is used to help reduce anxiety that may cause nervousness or behavior problems. It does not begin to help immediately. The full effect may not appear for 3-4 weeks.

Brand Name	Generic Name
BuSpar	Buspirone

What side effects might be seen from this medicine?

This medicine is usually very safe when used for short periods of time as the doctor prescribes. Sometimes antianxiety medicines seem to work backward, causing excitement, irritability, anger, aggression, trouble sleeping, nightmares, uncontrollable behavior, or memory loss. Contact parents immediately if this is noticed. BuSpar may cause dizziness, nervousness, nausea, headache, restlessness, or trouble sleeping but does not cause dependence or sleepiness.

What could happen if this medicine is stopped suddenly?

Many medicines cause problems if stopped suddenly. Stopping slowly is a good idea to see if the anxiety recurs.

Beta Blockers

What are Beta-Blockers?

Beta-Blockers have been used primarily to treat high blood pressure and irregular heartbeat. Recently, however, these medications have been used to treat emotional and behavior problems.

How can these medicines help?

Several studies of children and adolescents have shown that beta-blockers are effective in decreasing aggressive or violent behavior. These drugs may be particularly useful for patients who have developmental delays or autism. Beta-Blockers may reduce the aggression and anger that sometimes follow brain injuries. These medicines may also reduce some symptoms of anxiety and help children and adolescents who have experienced very frightening events or have posttraumatic stress disorder.

What are the common Beta-Blockers used?

Brand Name	Generic Name
Inderal	propranolol
Tenormin	atenolol
Visken	pindolol
Corgard	nadolol

How do these medicines work?

When beta-blockers are prescribed for patients with anxiety, aggression, or other behavior problems, these medicines stop the effect of certain chemicals on nerves in the body and possibly in the brain that are causing the symptoms. For example, beta-blockers decrease the anxiety symptoms of shaking, sweating, and rapid heartbeat.

What side effects can these medicines have?

Occasional side effects
* Tingling, numbness, or pain in the fingers
* Tiredness or weakness
* Slow heartbeat
* Low blood pressure
* Dizziness, (especially when standing up quickly; advise student to stand slowly)

Serious side effects
* Wheezing
* Sadness or irritability
* Hallucinations
* Muscle Cramps

Uncommon, but possible, side effects
* Nausea
* Trouble sleeping or nightmares
* Diarrhea
* Skin rash

What happens if these medicines are stopped suddenly?

Stopping Beta-Blockers suddenly may cause a fast or irregular heartbeat, high blood pressure, and severe emotional problems. Beta-Blockers should be discontinued gradually over a period of at least 2 weeks under a doctor's supervision.

How long will these medicines be needed?

The length of time the student will need to take beta-blockers depends on how well the medicine works for him or her and whether any side effects occur. Sometimes the student may need treatment lasting for several months.

4.- Catapres (Clonidine) and Tenex (Guanfacine)

What are Catapres and Tenex?

Catapres (clonidine) and Tenex (guanfacine) were first used to treat high blood pressure. Now they are being used to treat symptoms of Tourette's disorder, chronic tics, and attention deficit/hyperactivity disorder (ADHD). They are occasionally used to treat aggression, posttraumatic stress disorder, anxiety, panic disorder, and bipolar (manic-depressive) disorder in children and adolescents. Both medicines are available as pills. Catapres also comes in a skin patch that releases medicine slowly for 5 days.

How can these medicines help?

Catapres and Tenex can decrease symptoms of hyperactivity, impulsivity, anxiety, irritability, temper tantrums, explosive anger, conduct problems, and tics. They can increase patience and frustration tolerance, as well as improve self-control and cooperation with adults. These medicines are sometimes used with Ritalin (methylphenidate) or Dexedrine (dextroamphetamine) for ADHD or with Haldol (haloperidol) or Orap (pimozide) for Tourette's disorder. The positive effects usually do not start for 2 weeks after a stable dose is reached. The full benefit may not be seen for 2-4 months.

How do these medicines work?

Catapres and Tenex work by decreasing the level of excitement in part of the brain. This effect helps people with tic disorders to stop moving or making noises when they do not want to. It also helps children with ADHD to slow down and think before acting. These medications are not sedatives or tranquilizers, even though they may seem that way because they can make the student sleepy when he or she first starts taking them.

What side effects might be seen from these medicines?

Common side effects, especially at first
* Slow pulse rate
* Temporary worsening of tics in Tourette's
* Trouble sleeping
* Ringing ears
* Skin redness and itching under the skin patch

Less common side effects
* Depression
* Confusion
* Bed-wetting
* Muscle cramps
* Itching
* Runny Nose

Common side effects, if dosage is increased

* Sleepiness, especially when bored
* Low blood pressure
* Fatigue or tiredness
* Mild dizziness or light-headedness
* Stomachache

Serious, but uncommon side effects

* Severe or increased dizziness
* Sleepiness that worsens

Serious, but very rare, side effects

* Fainting
* Trouble breathing
* Sudden headaches
* Legs and feet swelling
* Irregular heartbeat
* Kidney Failure
* Vomiting and nausea

What could happen if these medicines are stopped suddenly?

If Catapres and Tenex are stopped suddenly, the following effects could result

* Very high blood pressure, even if blood pressure was normal before starting meds
* Temporary worsening of behavior problems or tics
* Nervousness, anxiety
* Rapid or irregular heartbeat
* Chest pain
* Headache
* Stomach cramps, nausea, vomiting
* Trouble sleeping

Because of these effects, it is important not to stop these medications suddenly, but to decrease them slowly as directed by the doctor. It is especially important not to miss doses of these medicines, because withdrawal symptoms or heart or blood pressure problems may occur. If the student takes a dose at school, it is essential not to let the prescription run out. It is especially important not to miss any Catapres doses if Ritalin is also being used.

How long will these medications be needed?

There is no way to know how long a person will need to take these medicines. The parents, the doctor, and the teacher will work together to determine what is right for each child. Sometimes the medicine may be needed for only a few years, but some people may need it longer.

5.- Desyrel (Trazodone) and Serzone (Nefazodone)

What are Desyrel and Serzone?

Desyrel (trazodone) and Serzone (nefazodone) have been successfully used to treat depression in adults. Now these medicines are beginning to be used to treat emotional and behavior problems, including depression, insomnia, and disruptive behavior disorders in children and adolescents.

How do these medicines help?

Desyrel and Serzone can decrease depression, irritability, and aggression. They can help to fall asleep at night.

How do these medicines work?

People with emotional and behavior problems may have low levels of brain chemical called serotonin. Desyrel and Serzone are believed to help by increasing brain serotonin to more normal levels.

What side effects can these medications have?

More common side effects	*Less common, but serious, side effects*
✳ Drowsiness/sleepiness	✳ Rapid heartbeat
✳ Dry mouth	✳ Fainting
✳ Dizziness, light-headedness	✳ Vomiting
✳ Headache	✳ Fever, sore throat, infection signs
✳ Blurred vision	✳ Prolonged penile erection (in boys)
✳ Nausea	✳ Increased interest in sex (in girls)
✳ More frequent erections (in boys)	

How long will these medicines be needed?

These medicines may not reach their full effect for several weeks. Subsequently, the student may need to take this medicine for at least several months so that emotional or behavior problems do not recur.

6.- Effexor (Venlafaxine)

What is Effexor?

Effexor (venlafaxine) has been used successfully to treat depression and anxiety in adults. Now this medication is being used to treat emotional and behavior problems, including anxiety, depression, and troubles with attention in children and adolescents.

How can Effexor help?

Effexor can decrease depression, irritability, and anxiety. It has been used to improve attention in children and adults.

How does this medicine work?

People with emotional and behavior problems may have unbalanced levels of certain chemicals in the brain. Effexor helps to restore the balance of these chemicals.

What side effects might be seen from this medicine?

More common side effects
* Anxiety, nervousness
* Nausea, upset stomach
* Sleepiness, insomnia
* Decreased appetite
* Weight loss

Less common, but serious side effects
* Increased blood pressure
* Seizures (fits, convulsions

Occasional side effects
* Yawning
* Blurred vision
* Dry mouth
* Dizziness
* Constipation
* Sweating
* Lack of energy
* Trouble with sexual functioning

What could happen if this medication is stopped suddenly?

No known serious medical withdrawal effects occur if Effexor is stopped suddenly, but there may be uncomfortable feelings.

How long will this medication be needed?

Effexor may take several weeks to reach its full effect. Subsequently, the student may need to take the medication for at least several months so that the emotional or behavior problem does not recur.

7.- Lithium

What is Lithium

Lithium is a naturally occurring salt that is available in several different forms, including lithium carbonate tablets (Lithotabs) or capsules, (Eskalith or Lithonate), controlled-release capsules or tablets (Eskalith CR or Lithobid) and lithium citrate syrup.

How can these medicines help?

Lithium may be prescribed for bipolar (manic-depressive) disorder, certain types of depression, severe mood swings, and very serious aggression. It decreases mood swings, rage, and explosive aggression. It can reduce the frequency and severity of fighting or destroying property.

How does this medicine work?

Lithium acts by stabilizing nerve cells in the brain. This affects behavior in different ways depending on the problem that is being treated. For children with bipolar disorder, it works by evening out the mood. For children with explosive aggression caused by rage, Lithium works by "running down" the rage and decreasing the impulsivity. The student then has time to figure out more constructive ways to deal with his or her rage. Finally, for children and adolescents with depression whose symptoms have not responded to standard, single-drug therapy, Lithium can make the antidepressant work better.

What side effects might be seen from Lithium?

Whenever possible, Lithium should be taken with food to decrease side effects. The side effects of Lithium are increased if a person is dehydrated. If side effects appear, try giving the student one or two glasses of water. Soft drinks with caffeine may worsen side effects.

Common side effects
(Often goes away after 2 weeks)

* Weight gain
* Stomachache
* Diarrhea
* Nausea, vomiting
* Increased thirst
* Increased frequency of urination
* Shakiness of hands
* Tiredness, weakness
* Headache
* Dizziness

Occasional side effects

* Low thyroid function or goiter
* Acne
* Skin rashes
* Hair loss
* Changes in blood sugar
* Metallic taste in mouth
* Irritability

Signs that Lithium level may be too high	Serious effects of too much Lithium Get medical care IMMEDIATELY
❋ Vomiting or diarrhea more than once	❋ Irregular heartbeat
❋ Worsening of or severe trembling	❋ Fainting
❋ Weakness	❋ Staggering
❋ Lack of coordination	❋ Blurred vision
❋ Unsteadiness when standing or walking	❋ Ringing sound in the ears
❋ Extreme sleepiness or tiredness	❋ Lack of urination
❋ Severe dizziness	❋ Muscle twitches
❋ Trouble speaking, slurred speech	❋ High fever
	❋ Seizures (fits, convulsions)
	❋ Unconsciousness

Overdosing with Lithium may cause DEATH.
This medication must be closely supervised at all times!

What could happen if this medicine is stopped suddenly?

No adverse medical withdrawal effects occur right away if Lithium is stopped suddenly. Some patients with bipolar disorder may become manic more often and be even more difficult to treat if Lithium is stopped suddenly. If the student has been taking Lithium for 6-8 weeks or longer, the dosage should be decreased gradually over 8-16 weeks before stopping in order to prevent this effect from happening.

How long will this medicine be needed?

For children and adolescents with bipolar disorder, Lithium is often prescribed for up to 2 years. Depending on how many times the student has had depression or mania, he or she may need to take the medicine indefinitely. Some patients do require Lithium throughout their entire life to function normally. For rage, Lithium must be continued for several months to years until the student, his or her family, and the doctor can find different ways to control the rage. Finally, for children and adolescents with severe depression who need Lithium along with an antidepressant, Lithium is usually needed for at least 5-6 months after the child's mood returns to normal. This is necessary to prevent the depression from recurring.

8.- Neuroleptics

What are neuroleptics?

Neuroleptics are a group of medicines also called antipsychotic medicines. They used to be called major tranquilizers.

How can these medicines help?

Neuroleptics are used to treat psychosis, such as schizophrenia, mania, or very severe depression. They may also be used for behavior problems after a head injury. They can reduce hallucinations and delusions and help the student be less upset and agitated. They can improve the ability to think clearly. Neuroleptics are also used to reduce motor and vocal tics and behavior problems in persons with Tourette's disorder. Sometimes they are used to reduce severe aggression or very serious behavior problems in young people with conduct disorder, mental impairments, or autism. These medicines are very powerful and are used to treat very serious problems or symptoms that do not respond to other medications. It is important to be patient. The positive effects of these medicines may not appear for 2-3 weeks.

What are the common neuroleptics used?

Brand Name	Generic Name
✳ Clozaril	✳ clozapine
✳ Haldol	✳ haloperidol
✳ Loxitane	✳ loxapine
✳ Mellaril	✳ thioridazine
✳ Moban	✳ molindone
✳ Navane	✳ thiothixene
✳ Orap	✳ pimozide
✳ Prolixin	✳ fluphenazine
✳ Risperdal	✳ risperidone
✳ Stelazine	✳ trifluoperazine
✳ Thorazine	✳ chlorpromazine
✳ Trilafon	✳ perphenazine
✳ Zyprexa	✳ olanzapine

How do these medication work?

One of the ways that the brain works is by creating substances called transmitters. Symptoms may be caused by too much or too little of these substances of problems with the area of the brain that should receive the transmitters. Neuroleptics work on these transmitters and the areas of the brain the receive them so that the symptoms are reduced.

What side effects might be seen from these medications?

Common, but not usually serious, side effects

* Dry mouth (allow student to chew sugar-free gum or drink extra water)
* Sleepiness or tiredness
* Constipation (allow student to drink more fluids or to use the bathroom)
* Mild trouble urinating
* Blurred vision
* Dizziness (this may happen in the classroom or during physical education)
* Weight gain
* Changes in menstrual cycle
* Increase in breast size (in boys and girls)
* Drooling
* Sadness, nervousness, clingingness, not wanting to go to school
* Increased risk of sunburn

Less common, but potentially serious, side effects

* Restlessness or inability to sit still
* Stiffness of tongue, jaw, neck, back, or legs
* Shakiness of hands and fingers (may be noticed as a worsening of handwriting)
* Overheating or heatstroke
* Seizures

Serious, but rare, side effect

* Decrease in number of blood cells or damage to the liver
* Extreme stiffness or lack of movement, very high fever, mental confusion
* Sudden stuffiness, inability to breathe or swallow

Most side effects diminish over time. Some can be reduced by decreasing the amount of medicine taken, by stopping the medicine, or by adding another medicine to combat the side effects. One side effect that may not go away is tardive dyskinesia (TD). Patients with tardive dyskinesia have involuntary movements of the body especially the mouth and tongue. Jerky movements of the arms, legs, or body may occur. If you notice anything like this, be sure to inform the child's parents.

Medicines used to treat the side effects of neuroleptics

Brand Name	Generic Name	Brand Name	Generic Name
Symmetrel	amantadine	Benedryl	diphenhydramine
Cogentin	benztropine mesylate	Artane	trihexyphenidyl
Akineton	biperiden	Inderal	propranolol
Catapres	clonidine	Ativan	lorazepam
Klonopin	clonazepam		

9.- Selective Serotonin Reuptake Inhibitors (SSRIs)

What are SSRIs?

SSRIs is a relatively new group of medicines. They have been used successfully to treat emotional and behavior problems, including depression, panic disorder, obsessive-compulsive disorder (OCD), bulimia, and posttraumatic stress disorder in adults. Now these medicines are being used to treat the same problems in children and adolescents.

What are the common SSRIs used?

Brand Name	Generic Name
❊ Luvox	❊ fluvoxamine
❊ Paxil	❊ paroxetine
❊ Prozac	❊ fluoxetine
❊ Zoloft	❊ sertraline

How do these medicines work?

Serotonin is a chemical that is naturally found in the brain. Low levels of brain serotonin are associated with emotional and behavior problems. SSRIs help people by increasing the levels of brain serotonin to more normal levels.

What side effects can these medicines have?

More common side effects

❊ Nausea, upset stomach (student may need to take medicine after a meal or snack)
❊ Diarrhea
❊ Headache
❊ Anxiety or nervousness
❊ Insomnia (difficulty falling asleep)
❊ Restlessness
❊ Dry mouth (allow student to chew sugar-free gum or take extra drinks of water)
❊ Sleepiness or tiredness
❊ Dizziness (tell student to try standing up slowly)
❊ Tremor (shakiness)
❊ Excessive sweating
❊ Apathy, lack of interest

Less common side effects

❊ Weight loss
❊ Increased activity, rapid speech, feeling "speeded up" being very excited or irritable
❊ Weight gain

Serious side effects

❊ Rash, hives, or heatstroke (prevent by decreasing activity in hot weather), seizures

What could happen if these medicines are stopped suddenly?

No known serious medical withdrawal effects occur if SSRIs are stopped suddenly, but there may be uncomfortable feelings, such as trouble sleeping or even seeing things that are not there, especially for Paxil. Because Prozac is particularly long acting, an occasional missed dose is of less concern than with the other SSRIs.

How long will these medicines be needed?

SSRIs may take several weeks to reach their full effect. Subsequently, the student may need to take the medicine for at least several months so that the emotional or behavior problem does not recur.

10.- Stimulants

What are stimulants?

Stimulants are medicines that can improve attention span, decrease distractibility, increase ability to finish things, improve ability to follow directions, decrease hyperactivity, and improve ability to think before acting (decrease impulsivity). Handwriting and completion of schoolwork and homework can improve. Fighting and stubbornness in youngsters with attention-deficit/hyperactivity disorder can decrease. If stimulants do not work or cause problematic side effects, other medicines can be used.

What are the common stimulants used?
Listed in order of how often they are prescribed

Brand Name	Generic Name
❋ Ritalin	❋ methylphenidate
❋ Dexedrine	❋ dextroamphetamine
❋ Cylert	❋ pemoline
❋ Adderall	❋ mixture of amphetamines
❋ Desoxyn Gadumet tablet	❋ methamphetamine

How do these medicines work?

In children and adolescents who have ADHD, stimulant medicines stimulate parts of the brain that are not working as well as they should. An example would be the part that controls impulsive actions ("the brakes"). These medicines are not tranquilizers or sedatives. They work in the same way in children and adults.

How long do these medicines last?

The effects of Ritalin and Dexedrine usually last 3-4 hours. Thus, symptoms may return in the late morning or late in the day. The longer-acting medicines, such as Ritalin Sustained-Release (SR) tablets, Dexedrine Spansule capsules, Cylert and Desoxyn Gradume tablets, have effects that last as long as 6-8 hours.

What side effects can these medicines have?

Common side effects

❋ Lack of appetite and weight loss (give medicine during or after meals not before)
❋ Insomnia (this may be the ADHD coming back rather than a side effect)
❋ Headaches
❋ Stomachaches
❋ Irritability, crankiness, crying, emotional sensitivity
❋ Loss of interest in friends
❋ Staring into space
❋ Rapid pulse rate or increased blood pressure

Less common side effects

❋ Rebound (as the medicine is wearing off, hyperactivity or bad mood may intensify)
❋ Slowing of growth (this is why the height and weight are checked regularly, growth usually catches up if the medicine is stopped or the dose is decreased)
❋ Nervous habits (such as picking at skin) or stuttering

Serious, but rare, side effect

❋ Motor or vocal tics (fast repeated movement or sounds)
❋ Muscle twitches (jerking movements) of parts of the body
❋ Sadness that lasts more than a few days
❋ Auditory, visual, or tactile hallucinations (hearing, seeing, or feeling things not there)
❋ Any behavior that is very unusual for the student

What happens if these medicines are stopped suddenly?

No medical withdrawal effects occur if stimulants are stopped suddenly. A few young people may experience irritability, trouble sleeping, or increased hyperactivity for a day or two if they have been taking medicine every day for a long time, especially at high doses. It may be better to decrease the medicine slowly over a week or so.

How long will these medicines be needed?

There is no way to know for certain how long a person will need to take these medicines. The parents, doctors, and teachers will work together to determine what is right for each young person. Sometimes the medicine is needed for only a few years, but some people may need to take medicine even as adults.

Other things to know about these medicines:

Stimulants do not cause illegal drug use or addiction. However, because the patient or other people may abuse these medicines, adult supervision is important. Some young people take the medicine three or four times a day, every day. Others need to take it only twice a day, on school days.

It is important for the student not to chew Ritalin-SR tablets or Dexedrine Spansule capsules because this releases too much medicine all at once.

11.- Tricyclic Antidepressants

What are Tryicyclic Antidepressants?

Tricyclic antidepressants were first used to treat depression, but are now also used to treat enuresis (bed wetting), attention-deficit hyperactivity disorder, school phobia, separation anxiety, panic disorder, obsessive-compulsive disorder (OCD), some sleep disorders (such as night terrors,) and trichotillomania (compulsive pulling out of one's hair) in children and adolescents.

How can these medicines help?

Tricyclic antidepressants can decrease depression, anxiety, panic, obsessions and compulsions, bed-wetting, night terrors or sleepwalking, and symptoms of ADHD. Each medicine in this group is better for some symptoms than for others. When treating enuresis, the medicine works right away. When treating depression, the medicine may take several weeks to work.

What are the common Tricyclic antidepressants used?
Listed in order of how often they are prescribed.

Brand Name	Generic Name
✳ Tofranil	✳ imipramine
✳ Pamelor or Aventyl	✳ nortiptyline
✳ Norpramin or Pertofrane	✳ desipramine
✳ Elavil or Endep	✳ amitriptyline
✳ Anafranil	✳ clomipramine

How do these medicines work?

When tricyclic antidepressants are prescribed for people with depression, these medicines affect the natural substances that are needed for certain parts of the brain to work more normally. For instance, the parts of the brain that regulate concentration, motivation, or mood will work better with help from these medicines.

What side effects can these medicines have?

Common side effects
* Dry mouth (allow student to chew sugar-free gum or to have extra drinks of water)
* Constipation (allow student to drink more fluids and use the bathroom often)
* Dizziness (remind student to stand up slowly)
* Weight gain
* Loss of appetite or weight loss (give medicine during or after meals, not before)
* Sleepiness
* Irritability

Occasional side effects

* Nightmares
* Stuttering
* Increased risk of sunburn (make sure student is wearing sunblock)
* Increase in breast size and nipple discharge (in girls)
* Increase in breast size (in boys)

Less common side effects

* High or low blood pressure
* Nausea (student may need to take medicine after a meal or snack)
* Trouble urinating
* Blurred vision (student may have difficulty seeing the chalkboard)
* Motor tics (fast repeated movements)
* Muscle twitches (jerking movements) of parts of the body
* Increased activity, rapid speech, feeling "speeded up"
* Decreased need for sleep, being very excited or irritable (cranky)

Rare, but potentially serious, side effects
Call parents immediately

* Seizures
* Very fast, irregular heartbeat
* Fainting
* Hallucinations (hearing voices or seeing things that are not there)
* Rash
* Inability to urinate
* Confusion
* Severe change in behavior

What could happen if these medicines are stopped suddenly?

Stopping the medicine or skipping a dose is not dangerous but can be very uncomfortable. It may feel like coming down with the flu (having a headache, muscle aches, stomachache, and upset stomach) Behavior problems, sadness, nervousness, or trouble sleeping may occur. If these feelings appear daily, the medicine may need to be given more often during each day.

How long will these medicines be needed?

There is no way to know for certain how long a person will need to take these medicines. The parents, doctors, and teachers will work together to determine what is right for each child.

12.- Wellbutrin (bupropion)

What is wellbutrin (bupropion)?

Wellbutrin (bupropion) has been used successfully to treat depression in adults. Now this medicine is beginning to be used to treat emotional and behavior problems, including depression, attention-deficit hyperactivity disorder, and conduct problems in children and adolescents.

How can this medicine help?

Wellbutrin can decrease depression, impulsive behavior, and aggression.

How does this medicine work?

Wellbutrin helps people by normalizing the levels of certain chemicals that are naturally found in the brain.

What side effects can this medicine have?

Most common side effects

* Nervousness, restlessness
* Dry mouth (allow student to chew sugar-free gum or to get extra drinks of water)
* Constipation (allow student to drink more fluids and use the bathroom often)
* Headache
* Weight loss
* Nausea (student may need to take medicine after a meal or snack)
* Dizziness (remind student to stand up slowly)
* Excessive sweating

Occasional side effects

* Motor tics (fast, repeated movements)
* Muscle twitches (jerking movements) of parts of the body
* Trouble sleeping
* Rash
* Swelling around the mouth

Less common, but more serious, side effects

* Vomiting
* Seizures (fits, convulsion)
* Unusual excitement
* Decreased need for sleep
* Rapid speech

Peytral Publications Inc.

What could happen if this medicine is stopped suddenly?

No known medical withdrawal effects occur if Wellbutrin is stopped suddenly. Some people may get a headache as the medicine wears off. If the medicine is stopped, the original problems may recur. Parents should consult the doctor before stopping the medicine with their child.

How long will this medicine be needed?

Wellbutrin may take several weeks to reach its full effect. Subsequently, the student may need to take the medicine for at least several months so that the emotional or behavior problem does not recur.

Other information about this medicine:

It can be very dangerous to take Wellbutrin at the same time as, or even within several weeks of, taking another type of medicine called a monomania oxides inhibitor.

Section V

Teacher Resources

Attention Deficit Disorder (ADD)
Attention Deficit Hyperactivity Disorder (ADHD)

Websites

www.chadd.org
Children and Adults with Attention Deficit/Hyperactivity Disorder (CHADD)

www.mental-health-matters.com/add.html
Hyperactivity and Attention Deficit Hyperactivity Disorder, ADD, ADHD

www.cdipage.com
About Attention Deficit Hyperactivity Disorder, ADD

www.mentalhealth.com/dis/fr20.html
Attention-Deficit Hyperactivity Disorder

Resource Books

Attention Without Tension:
A Teacher's Handbook on Attention Disorders.
Copeland, Edna D & Love, Valerie L. 1995, 178 pp. 2nd Ed.
Specialty Press, Incorporated.
Practical information and ideas to use in the class when teaching children with ADD and ADHD.

Everything you need to know about ADD/ADHD.
Beal, Eileen. 1998, 64 pp. The Rosen Publishing Group, Incorporated.
Defines ADD and ADHD, and discusses what can be done to treat the conditions, including medication, behavior modification, and counseling.

Pants with Pockets and Other Tips on Managing an ADD/ADHD Child.
Matos, Candi & Matos, Chris. 1999, 138 pp. 2nd Ed. The Herbal Way.
Provides practical strategies and tips on effectively handling children with ADD and ADHD.

Attention Deficit Disorder/ ADHD and ADD Syndromes.
Jordan, Dale R. 1998, 202 pp. 3rd Ed. Pro-Ed International Publisher.
This book is useful and appropriate for both parents and teachers who are searching for creative ways to be more successful in the treatment of ADHD and ADD.

How to Reach and Teach ADD/ADHD Children.
Rief, Sandra, 1995, 256 pp. The Center for Applied Research in Education.
A helpful guide full of practical techniques, strategies, and interventions for helping children with attention problems and hyperactivity.

Coping with ADD/ADHD
Morrison, Jaydene, 1997, 93pp. Hazelden Information and Educational Services.
Easy-to-understand information which helps children with ADD/ADHD to understand the disorder and provides practical assistance in how to cope with the effects of ADD/ADHD.

Why Johnny Can't Concentrate:
Coping with Attention Deficit Problems
Moss, Robert A. & Dunlap, Helen H. 1990, 225 pp. Bantam Books, Incorporated.
This book is helpful for parents to gain an understanding of what their children are feeling. This book will provide Information to parents, to help them to become informed advocates for their children, shielding them from public humiliation and to sustain their self-esteem.

Children's Picture Books

Eddie Enough!
Zimmett, Debbie. 2001, 48 pp. Woodbine House.
Third-grader Eddie Minetti is described as a human whirlwind. He is always getting into trouble at school until his AD/HD is diagnosed and treated.

Eukee the Jumpy, Jumpy Elephant.
Corman, Clifford & Trevino, Esther. 1995, 22 pp. Specialty Press, Incorporated.
This is the story of a young elephant's struggle with attention deficit disorder. Eukee gets into trouble at home and school because he can't sit still and follow directions. He gets help at home and from a special doctor and learns ways to succeed.

Shelley: The Hyperactive Turtle
Moss, Deborah M. 1989, 19 pp. Woodbine House.
After his mother takes him to the doctor, Shelley the turtle begins to understand why he feels so jumpy and wiggly inside that he can't sit still.

Zipper, the Kid with ADHD
Janover, Caroline & Powell, Rick (ill). 1997, 108 pp. Woodbine House.
Zipper is a fifth-grader who is always getting into trouble at home and school due to his impulsive behaviors. He has trouble concentrating and controlling himself until he finds a new talent and someone who believes in him, giving him a new motivation to try harder.

Anxiety

Websites

www.adaa.org
ADAA - Anxiety Disorders Association of America

www.anxietypanic.com
Anxiety/Panic Attack Resource Site

www.anxiety-relief.com
Anxiety-Relief Center

www.anxietynetwork.com
Anxiety Network International

Resource Books

Anxiety Disorders in Children and Adolescents
March, John S. 1995, 448 pp. Guilford Publications Inc.
A collection of papers about anxiety disorders in children and adolescents. Provides information of the recognition and treatment of childhood-onset anxiety syndromes.

A Handbook of Childhood Anxiety Management
Dwivedi, Kedar N (ed.) & Varma, Ved (ed.). 1997, 252 pp, Ashgate Publishing Company.
This book addresses the causes, nature, and distribution of anxiety problems in children and offers various approaches to treatment. It is aimed at assisting professionals in offering skillful help to children.

Autism

Websites

www.mhsource.com/hy/autism.html
Autism Fact Sheet

www.teacch.com
Autism Primer - Twenty Questions

www.autism.org
Center for the Study of Autism

www.autism.com
Autism Research Institute

Resource Books

Learning and Cognition in Autism
Schopler, Eric; Mesibov, Gary. 1995, 346 pp. Perseus Publishing.
An introduction to cognitive approaches to understanding and working with people with autism. This book covers cognitive and social deficits and intervention strategies, verbal and nonverbal cognitive processes, motivating communication in autistic children, social cognition, and educational strategies.

Teaching Children with Autism: Strategies for Initiating Positive Interactions and Improving Learning Opportunities.
Koegel, Robert L.; Koegel, Lynn K. 1995, 236 pp. Paul H. Brooks.
This positive, research based text dispels the stereotypes surrounding autism by providing accurate information on how much children with this complex disorder can learn.

Autism Treatment Guide
Gerlach, Elizabeth. 1996, 130 pp. Four Leaf Press.
This book is written by a mother of a child with autism. It offers information on the treatments currently available for autism.

Activity Schedules for Children with Autism.
McClannahan, Lynn; Krantz, Patricia J. 1999, 117 pp. Woodbine House.
This book is a great resource for parents and teachers of children with autism as it provides detailed explanations and examples of activity schedules. It demonstrates how effectively activity schedules can foster greater independence and social awareness in the daily lives of children with autism.

Autism: Information and Resources for Parents, Families and Professionals
Simpson, Richard L.; Zionts, Paul. 1992, 172 pp. Pro-Ed.
This book is set up in a question-answer format for parents and families, to answer many of the most commonly asked questions about autism.

Autism: The Facts
Baron-Cohen, Simon; Bolton, Patrick. 1993, 113 pp. Oxford University Press, Incorporated.
A book for parents and educators explaining what is known about autism, from the scientific point of view.

Reaching Out, Joining In
Weiss, Mary Jane; Harris, Sandra L. 2001, 150 pp. Woodbine House.
An excellent guide for parents and teachers to utilize when assisting students with autism in becoming better socially adjusted at home and at school.

Right from the Start
Harris, Sandra L.; Weiss, Mary Jane. 1998, 138 pp. Woodbine House.
An informative guide for both parents and teachers of children with autism. It provides behavioral intervention ideas to utilize for young children with autism.

The Hidden Child
Simons, Jeanne; Oishi, Sabine. 1987, 286 pp. Woodbine House.
A guidebook for teachers and therapists which utilizes the Linwood Method for reaching the autistic child. The linwood Method provides an informative look at autism as well as a uniquely successful treatment program for the autistic child

Children's Picture Books

Andy and His Yellow Frisbee
Thompson, Mary. 1996, 20 pp. Woodbine House.
This book tells the story of a new girl at school who tries to befriend Andy, an autistic boy, who spends every recess by himself.

Russell is Extra Special: A Book about Autism in Children
Amenta, Charles A. III. 1992, 15 pp. American Psychological Association
This book was written to help children learn about autism. The author is a father of an autistic child as well as a physician. Parents, teachers, and other professionals will find this book very helpful.

Mori's Story: A Book About a Boy with Autism
Gartenberg, Zachary & Gay, Jerry (ill.) 1998, 40 pp. The Lerner Publishing Group.
A young boy discuss his home life and schooling with his autistic brother, Mori. He discusses how his family learned that Mori was autistic, the kinds of treatment Mori receives, and how it affects all of their lives.

Bi-Polar (Manic Depression)

Websites

www.psycom.net/depression.central.bipolar.html
 Bipolar Disorder --- Manic Depression

www.telusplanet.net/public/synergy
 Mental Health Research Site

www.bipolar.com
 Bipolar Website

Resource Books

The Bipolar Child: The Definitive and Reassuring Guide to Childhood's Most Misunderstood Disorder, Vol. 1
Papolos, Demitri F. & Papolos, Janice. 1999, 398 pp. Broadway Books.
This book is about early-onset bipolar disorder. Bipolar disorder was once thought to be rare in children; however, researchers are now discovering that not only can bipolar disorder begin very early in life, but it is also much more common than ever imagined. This book asks "Why is this illness often misdiagnosed or overlooked?"

Bronchopulmonary Dysplasia

Websites

www.cheo.on.ca/bpd/BPDindx.html
Bronchopulmonary Dysplasia: Information for parents on BPD

www.lungusa.org/diseases/bpdfac.html
Bronchopulmonary Dysplasia Fact Sheet

Cerebral Palsy

Websites

www.irsc.org/cerebral.htm
Cerebral Palsy (CP)

www.miller-dwan.com
Cerebral Palsy and Spaciticity

www.familyvillage.wisc.edu/lib_cerp.htm
The Family Village / Library / Cerebral Palsy

www.geocities.com/Athens/Thebes/6822
Cerebral Palsy

Resource Books

Coping with Cerebral Palsy: Answers to Questions Parents Often Ask
Schleichkorn, Jay. 1996, 252 pp. 2nd Ed. Pro-Ed International Publisher.
In this book, questions most frequently asked by parents are answered. Information is obtained by searching the literature, talking with professional personnel, meeting with parents, and talking to adults with cerebral palsy.

Children with Cerebral Palsy: A Parent's Guide
Geralis, Elaine. 1998, 424 pp. 2nd Ed. Woodbine House.
This book is a complete and compassionate guide to everything parents need to know about raising their child with cerebral palsy and meeting their varied medical, therapeutic, and educational needs.

Everything You Need to Know about Cerebral Palsy
Pincus, Dion. 1999, 64 pp. Rosen Publishing Group.
This book begins with a description of the characteristics or symptoms that constitute the condition or physical disability. It also discusses the causes, both known and speculated. The medical treatments, schooling, and family life of individuals with these conditions are also discussed. The language in this book is simple, with medical terms explained both in the text and in the glossary.

Children's Picture Books

Taking Cerebral Palsy to School
Anderson, Elizabeth Mary; Gosselin, Kim (ed) & Dineen, Tom (ill.) 2000, 32pp. JayJo Books, L L C.
This book is written from the perspective of a child with CP. It answers many of the questions his classmates have, but are too scared to ask. Children, teachers, school nurses, parents, and caregivers will all learn about CP.

I'm the Big Sister Now
Emmert, Michelle & Owens, Gail (ill.) 1991, 32 pp. Albert Whitman Publishing.
Nine year old Michelle describes the joys, difficulties, and other special situations involved in living with her older sister Amy, who was born severely disabled with cerebral palsy.

Howie Helps Himself
Fassler, Joan & Lasker, Joe (ill.) 1991, 29 pp. Albert Whitman Publishing
Howie, a boy with cerebral palsy, enjoys life and loves his famil; however, he wants more than anything to be able to move his wheelchair himself.

Chronic Fatigue Syndrome

Websites

www.cdc.gov/ncidod/diseases/cfs/index.htm
   Chronic Fatigue Syndrome Home Page

www.immunesupport.com
   Chronic Fatigue Syndrome and Fibromyalgia Resource

www.aacfs.org
   The American Association for Chronic Fatigue Syndrome - AACFS

Resource Books

Chronic Fatigue Syndrome: The Hidden Epidemic *Stoff, Jesse A; Pellegrino, Charles R.; & Geiss, Tony. 1992, 384 pp. Harper Trade.* This book explains the difficult to diagnose and impossible to "cure", Chronic Fatigue Syndrome.   It is considered a breakthrough guide for anyone sick and tired of feeling sick and tired.

Running on Empty: The Complete Guide to Chronic Fatigue Syndrome *Berne, Katrina H. 1995, 315 pp. (2nd ed.) Hunter House, Incorporated.* This book offers a definition of CFS as well as the history, symptoms, and effects this has on patients' lives. The book discusses options of treatment as well as ways to cope with CFS.

Conduct Disorders

Websites

www.klis.com/chandler/pamphlet/oddcd/oddcdpamphlet.htm
Oppositional Defiant Disorder (ODD) and Conduct Disorder (CD) in Children and Adolescents.

www.mentalhealth.com/dis/p20-ch02.html
Conduct Disorder

www.athealth.com/Practitioner/Newsletter/FPN_3_7.html
Disruptive Behavior Disorders

www.noah-health.org/english/illness/mentalhealth/mental.html
Fact Sheet: Oppositional Defiant Disorder (ODD)

Resource Books

Complete Early Childhood Behavior Management Guide
Watkins, Kathleen P. & Durant, Lucius. 1997, 192 pp.
The Center for Applied Research in Education.
This guide provides insight and tools to obtain the best possible behavior from young children, as well as effective, child-tested strategies for resolving problem behaviors when they occur.

Conduct Disorders in Childhood and Adolescence, Vol. 9
Kazdin, Alan E. 1995, 200 pp (2nd ed) Sage Publications, Incorporated.
This book describes the nature of conduct disorder and what is now known based on recent research and clinical work. Discussion is also given to key risk factors of conduct disorders, treatments of conduct disorders, and prevention of conduct disorders.

Preventing Childhood Disorders, Substance Abuse, and Delinquency
Peters, Ray D. & McMahon, Robert J. (Ed) 1996, 364 pp.
Sage Publications Incorporated.
This book presents the results of recent research on early intervention programs with children from birth to adolescence. Among them are social skills training for children with conduct disorder, anger-coping groupwork for aggressive children, parent training programs, and programs for high risk children.

Cystic Fibrosis

Websites

www.cff.org
Cystic Fibrosis Foundation

cf-web.mit.edu
CF-WEB: Cystic Fibrosis Information Online

www.cysticfibrosis.co.uk/cystic.htm
Cystic Fibrosis Resource Centre

www.cfri.org
Cystic Fibrosis Research, Inc. (CFRI)

Resource Books

Understanding Cystic Fibrosis
Hopkins, Karen. 1998, 128 pp. University Press of Mississippi.
Cystic Fibrosis (CF) is the most common genetic disorder in the white population.
Understanding CF charts the progress that has been made in identifying the cause of CF.

A Parent's Guide to Cystic Fibrosis
Shapiro, P. L. & Heussner, Ralph C. 1990, 120 pp. University of Minnesota Press.
A clear and comprehensive guide written to help parents and professionals to understand the nature, cause and treatment of Cystic Fibrosis. The text is filled with comments from parents and patients and includes a chapter devoted to family life.

Children's Picture Books

Taking Cystic Fibrosis to School
Henry, Cynthia S., Gosselin, Kim (ed) & Dineen, Tom (ill.) 2000, 32 pp.
Jayjo Books, L L C
This book is written from the perspective of a child with cystic fibrosis to explain and educate her classmates about her condition. This book is designed to help kids, families, teachers, school nurses and caregivers to better understand cystic fibrosis.

Depression

Websites

www.depression-net.com
    Depression - Net, source of information on depression, including treatments and medicines.

www.bestsitez.com/depression
    Causes, varieties, symptoms and solutions to depression, mailing list, depression discussion board, online counselors and more.

www.hoptechno.com/book34.htm
    Depression: Define It. Defeat It.

Resource Books

Childhood Depression: School-Based Intervention
Stark, Kevin D. 1990, 234 pp. Guildford Publications, Incorporated.
This book provides information for school-based intervention techniques. This book is recommended for all school educators and counselors.

The Childhood Depression Sourcebook
Miller, Jeffry A. 1998, 267 pp. Lowell House.
This book provides resources for everything you need to know about diagnosing the symptoms of childhood depression, problems that may occur due to depression, (such as anxiety, ADD/ADHD, and substance abuse) and treatment methods, including psychotherapy.

Growing up Sad: Childhood Depression and its Treatment
Cytryn, Leon & McKnew, Donald H. 1998, 216 pp. Norton, Ww.
This book presents information on the advances in diagnosis and treatment of childhood depression. Characteristics of depression, environmental and biological causes, and treatment is discussed.

Help Me, I'm Sad
Fassler, David G. & Dumas, Lynne S. 1997, 224 pp. Viking Penguin.
A reassuring guide for parents of adolescents whose lives are darkened by depression. This book helps to recognize, treat, and prevent childhood and adolescent depression.

Down Syndrome

Websites

www.nas.com/downsyn
   Family Empowerment Network: A resource for families who have children with Down's Syndrome

www.downsnet.org
   DownsNet provides access to journal articles about Down Syndrome

www.dsrf.org
   Down Syndrome Foundation

www.nads.org
   National Association for Down Syndrome

Resource Books

Down Sydrome: The Facts
Selikowitz, Mark. 1990, 205 pp. Oxford University Press, Incorporated.
This book has been written for parents who have a child with Down Syndrome. It would also be of interest to friends, teachers, and therapists who come into contact with children with Down Syndrome.

Teaching Reading to Children with Down Syndrome:
A Guide for Parents and Teachers
Oelwein, Patricia L. 1995, 371 pp. Woodbine House
Children with Down Syndrome can be taught to read using an approach that provides for their unique learning styles and needs. This book describes a reading program that ensures success when tailored to meet the needs of each students.

Down Syndrome: Living and Learning in the Community
Nadel, Lynn (ed) & Rosenthal, Donna (ed). 1995, 297 pp.
Wiley, John and Sons, Incorporated.
This book provides information and advice about Down Syndrome including an overview of the latest medical advances and information about the programs and services now available.

Children's Picture Books

Our Brother has Down's Syndrome: An Introduction for Children
Cairo, Shelley: Cairo, Jasmine, et al. 1991, 10 pp. Firefly Books, LTD.
In this book, two sisters tell about their experience with having a little brother who has Down's Syndrome.

Where's Chimpy?
Rabe, Berniece & Schmidt, Diane. 1988, 13 pp. Albert Whitman
Text and photographs in this book show Misty, a little girl with Down Syndrome, and her father reviewing her day's activities in their search for her stuffed monkey.

Be Good to Eddie Lee
Fleming, Virginia & Cooper, Floyd (ill). 1997, 32 pp.
The Putnam Publishing Company.
Eddie Lee is a boy with Down Syndrome. Christy discovers special things about Eddie Lee, when Eddie Lee follows Christy into the woods.

Russ and the *Almost* Perfect Day
Rickert, Janet E. & McGahan, Pete (ill). 2001, 24 pp. Woodbine House.
Russ, a student with Down syndrome, is having a perfect day until he realizes that the five-dollar bill he has found probably belongs to a classmate.

Russ and the Firehouse
Rickert, Janet E. & McGahan, Pete (ill). 2000, 24 pp. Woodbine House.
Russ, a five-year-old with Down syndrome, visits his uncle's firehouse and gets to help with the daily chores.

We'll Paint the Octopus Red
Stuve-Bodeen, Stephanie & DeVito, Pam (ill). 1998, 28 pp. Woodbine House.
Emma and her father discuss what they will do when the new baby arrives, but they adjust their expectations when he is born with Down syndrome.

Epilepsy

Websites

www.efa.org
Epilepsy Foundation
www.epilepsynse.org.uk/pages/index/home/
National society for epilepsy

Resource Books

Epilepsy: Practical and Easy to Follow Advice
Marshall, Fiona. 1999, 146 pp. Element Books
This book looks at the effective treatments which can help reduce the intensity and frequency of seizures and increase control of a child's epilepsy. It also includes stress-management techniques and ways to help your child create a positive self-image.

Seizures and Epilepsy in Childhood: A Guide for Parents
Freeman, John M.; Pillas, Diana, J & Vining, Eileen P. 1997, 322 pp.
John Hopkins University Press.
This guide provides parents with the latest information about diagnosis, treatment, and the possible side effects of treatments, as well as practical advice about medication, decision-making, and risk- taking, which are all part of being the parent of a child with epilepsy.

A Guide to Understanding and Living with Epilepsy
Devinsky, Orrin. 1994, 345 pp. Davis F A
This book is an important and easy-to-understand resource for people with epilepsy and for their families. Both the newly diagnosed and those living with epilepsy will find valuable information on a wide range of medical, social, and legal issues

The Epilepsy Handbook: The Practical Management of Seizures
Gumnit, Robert J. 1994, 2nd ed. 194 pp. Lippincott-Raven Publishers.
A useful reference which provides an explanation of seizures and epilepsy, as well as treatment options for children and infants with epilepsy.

Children's Picture Books

Taking Seizure Disorders to School: A Story About Epilepsy
Gosselin, Kim & Freedman, Moss (ill). 1998, 32 pp. Jayjo Books, L L C
This picture book helps children to understand the condition of epilepsy.

Lee, The Rabbit with Epilepsy
Moss, Deborah M. & Schwartz, Carol (ill). 1990, 32 pp. Woodbine House.
Lee is diagnosed as having epilepsy, but medicine to control her seizures reduces her worries as she learns she can still lead a normal life.

Dotty the Dalmation has Epilepsy
Tim Peters Company Incorporated (Ed). 1996, 20pp.
Tim Peters & Company Incorporated.
This delightful story is about Dotty the Dalmatian who discovers she has epilepsy. At first, Dotty feels embarrassed and afraid. Once she accepts and learns how to control her seizures, she helps firefighters save lives. An excellent story for explaining epilepsy to children.

Fetal Alcohol Syndrome

Websites

www.nofas.org
Nofas Home Page

www.mel.lib.mi.us/health/health-fas.html
MEL: Fetal Alcohol Syndrome (FAS)

www.irsc.org/fas.htm
Internet Resources for Special Children (IRSC): Fetal Alcohol Syndrome/Effects

Resource Books

Born Substance Exposed, Educationally Vulnerable
Vicent, Lisbeth J., et al. 1991, 30 pp. Council for Exceptional Children.
This book examines what is known about the long term effects of exposure in- utero to alcohol and other drugs, as well as educational implications of those effects.

The Broken Cord
Dorris, Michael. 1989, 281 pp. HarperCollins Publishers Incorporated.
This is a story of a problem that is all around us today, Fetal Alcohol Syndrome and Fetal Alcohol Effects. It is a story of one family's life with a child of FAS. The book tries to open everyone's eyes to the completely preventable tragedy of children born with FAS and FAE.

Children of Prenatal Substance Abuse
Sparks, Shirley N. 1993, 177 pp. Singular Publishing Group, Inc.
Information is provided on substance abuse, addiction, biological and environmental risk factors, and physiological, mental health, and social outcomes. The author presents implications for working with families, including the effects of prenatal cocaine exposure on early childhood development, and assessment and intervention strategies for children affected by cocaine as infants, toddlers, and preschoolers. Also the effects of maternal alcohol use during pregnancy and effective interventions for children with Fetal Alcohol Syndrome or Fetal Alcohol Effects is presented.

What You Can Do to Prevent Fetal Alcohol Syndrome: A Professional's Guide

Blume, Sheila B. 1992, 58 pp. Hazelden Information and Educational Services.
This guide is designed to help professionals motivate clients to seek out early and adequate prenatal care, avoid all use of alcohol during pregnancy, explore ways to get help for alcohol and alcohol related problems, and make the birth of their babies a happy event.

Teaching Children Affected by Prenatal Drug Exposure

Seitz de Martinez, Barbara J. (Ed). 1995, 323 pp. Phi Delta Kappa Intl, Inc.
The purpose of this book is to provide educators with useful discussion of the facts and issues surrounding drug-exposed children in hope of facilitating a better understanding of these children and appropriate responses to their needs.

Fantastic Antone Succeeds

Kleinfeld, Judith & Wescott, Siobhan. 1996, 368 pp. University of Alaska Press.
This book brings together experienced teachers, professionals, and parents to explore the issue: How do we educate the alcohol-affected children whose numbers appear to be increasing in the schools? What can parents do in the home and what can educators do through the schools

---

Fragile X Syndrome

Websites

www.fraxsocal.org
    What is Fragile X?

www.fraxa.org
    FRAXA Research Foundation - Fragile X

www.nfxf.org
    The National Fragile X Foundation - Fragile X Syndrome

Resource Books

> ### Children with Fragile X Syndrome
> *Weber, Jayne D. (ed). 2000, 460 pp. Woodbine House*
> This book is the first of its kind and provides parents with a conclusiv, informative guide to Fragile X Syndrome.

Hunter Syndrome

Websites

members. aol.com/mpssociety/hunter.html
    MPS II - Hunter Syndrome

Klinefelter Syndrome

Websites

www.klinefeltersyndrome.org/index
    Klinefelter Syndrome Support Group website

www.nih.gov/health/chip/nichd/klinefelter/
    Understanding Klinefelter Syndrome

Learning Disabilities

Websites

www.ldonline.org
> LD OnLine: Learning Disabilities Infomration & Resources

www.ldanatl.org
> Learning Disabilities Association of America

www.ncld.org
> National Center for Learning Disabilities

www.nimh.nih.gov/publicat/learndis.htm
> Learning Disabilities

www.dyslexia.com
> Dyslexia: The Gift. Information and Resources for Dyslexia

Resource Books

The School Survival Guide for Kids with LD:
Ways to make learning easier and more fun.
Cummings, Rhoda; Fisher, Gary & Espeland, Pamela (ed.) 1991, 164 pp.
Free Spirit Publishing, Inc.
This book will help answer questions for students with learning disabilities.
It offers strategies and tips for building confidence in reading, writing, spelling, and math, managing time, coping with tests, and getting help. It also discusses how children with "learning differences" can get along better in school.

Teaching Study Strategies to Students with Learning Disabilities
Strichart, Stephen S.; Mangrum, Charles T. II. & Iannuzzi, Patricia. (2nd Ed.) 1993,
369 pp. Allyn & Bacon, Inc.
Teaching students with special needs to use study skills and strategies effectively is an important step in transforming these students into independent learners. This book includes more than 150 reproducible activities. These activities provide opportunities for active learning and student practice in the study skills and strategies most important for students with special needs in grades 4-12.

Educational Care: A System for Understanding and Helping Children with Learning Problems at Home and in School.
Levine, Melvin D. 1998, 325 pp. Educators Publishing Service, Incorporated.
This book provides useful strategies to try with students with disabilities to help them experience success in school.

Learning Disabilities: A to Z
Smith, Corinne & Strick, Lisa. 1999, 407 pp. Simon and Schuster Trade.
This book offers answers for parents of children who have neurological impairments affecting visual perception, language processing, fine motor skills, and the ability to focus attention.

The Survival Guide for Kids with LD
Fisher, Gary L.; Rhoda, Cummings; Nielsen, Nancy, J (ed) & Urbanovic, Jackie (ill). 1991, 96 pp. Free Spirit Publishing, Inc.
This is a useful handbook for kids with learning disabilities. The book discusses different types of disorders, programs at school, coping with negative feelings, and making friends. It also includes a section for parents and teachers.

The Learning Differences SourceBook
Boyles, Nancy & Contadino, Darlene. 1998, 480 pp. Lowell House.
For both parents and educators, this guide identifies and evaluates learning differences and various methods of providing the best home and school environment for a child with a learning difference.

Children's Picture Books

He's My Brother
Lasker, Joe. 1974, 38 pp. Albert Whitman.
A young boy describes the experiences of his slow learning younger brother at school and at home.

The Don't-Give-Up Kid and Learning Differences
Gehret, Jeanne. 1996, 3rd ed., 40 pp. Verbal Images Press.
As Alex becomes aware of his different learning style, he realizes his hero, Thomas Edison had similar problems.

Mental Impairments

Websites

www.thearc.org
> The Arc of the U.S. web site

www.thearc.org/faqs.htm
> Introduction to Mental Retardation

Resource Books

Teaching Students with Mental Retardation:
A Life Goal Curriculum Planning Approach
Thomas, Glen E. 1996, 597 pp. Prentice Hall
This book provides information regarding students with Mental Impairments and offers ideas to use when planning curriculum.

When Slow is Fast Enough: Educating the Delayed Preschool Child
Goodman, Joan F. 1995, 306 pp. Guildford Publications, Inc.
The author of this book offers a less directive model of instruction in which the educator's aim is to support the child's natural and spontaneous, albeit slow, development, and to stimulate individual processes of discovery and self-expression.

Mental Retardation: Nature, Cause and Management
Baroff, George & Olley, Gregory. 1999, (3rd ed) 497 pp. Brunner/Mazel Publishers.
This book is a new edition revisiting the major issues affecting individuals with mental retardation, those responsible for their education and well-being, and society at large. This book includes up-to-date information on the disorder & its management.

Children with Mental Retardation
Smith, Romayne, M.A. 1993, 437 pp. Wodbine House
A book for parents of children with mental retardation. It provides positive insight andl information regarding their child's medical, therapeutic, and educational needs. It gives parents an outlook they need to assist their child in reaching his or her highest potential.

Muscular Dystrophy

Websites

www.mdausa.org
Muscular Dystrophy Association (MDA) USA homepage

www.mdff.org
Muscular Dystrophy Family Foundation

www.mdausa.org/disease/index
Muscular Dystrophy Association/ Disease

Resource Books

> #### Muscular Dystrophy: The Facts
> *Emery, Alan E. H. 1994, 152 pp. Oxford University Press, Incorporated.*
> Muscular Dystrophy: The facts about living with Muscular Dystrophy and coping with its effects. This book will answer many of the questions that are often asked about how and why it occurs, and how it will affect the life of a recently diagnosed child.

> #### Muscular Dystrophy in Children: A Guide for Families
> *Siegle, Irwin M. 1999, 130 pp. Demos Medical Publishing Incorporated*
> This book is written for parents, friends, & educators of children who live with MD. It discusses common signs & symptoms & looks into the current treatment options available.

Children's Picture Books

> #### Martin the Hero Merriweather
> *Jackson, Bobby; Carter, Michael; & Fultz, Jim (ill). 1993, 49 pp.*
> *Multicultural Publications.*
> Because of his physical handicap, Martin struggles to gain acceptance from his classmates, and he finally proves to the whole community that he can even be a hero.

My Buddy

Osofsky, Audrey & Rand, Ted (ill). 1995, 54 pp. Houghton Mifflin Company.
A young boy with MD tells how he is teamed up with a dog trained to do things for him that he cannot do himself.

Schizophrenia

Websites

www.schizophrenia.com
> The Schizophrenia Home Page

www.mhsource.com/narsad
> National Alliance for Research on Schizophrenia and Depression

www.pslgroup.com/SCHIZOPHR.htm
> Schizophrenia - Doctor's Guide to the Internet

Resource Books

Childhood Schizophrenia
Cantor, Sheila. 1998, 193 pp. Guildford Publications, Inc.
This book presents 54 case histories of schizophrenic children and reveals the family histories that show increased prevalence in these families of other neuropsychiatric disorders, such as epilepsy and mental retardation. The physical characteristics associated with childhood schizophrenia are described.

Children without Childhood: A Study of Childhood Schizophrenia
Wolman, Benjamin B. 1970, 248 pp. Saunders WB Co.
This is a guide through child psychoses which provides useful and practical information for working with children with schizophrenia.

Coping with Schizophrenia: A Guide for Families
Mueser, Kim T. & Gingerich, Susan. 1994, 355 pp. New Harbinger Publications.
This book provides helpful strategies for coping with stress and other issues related to schizophrenia.

Seasonal Affective Disorders

Websites

www.mentalhealth.com/book/p40-sad.html
Seasonal Affective Disorder

www.athealth.com/Practitioner/Newsletter/FPN_3_2.html
Seasonal Affective Disorder - SAD

www.bio-light.com
Light Therapy for Seasonal Affective Disorder (SAD), Winter Depression: Light

Resource Books

Banishing the Blues of Seasonal Affective Disorder
Barr, Bruce C. 2000, 64 pp. Indoorsun.com Publishing.
A very clear and easy-to-read book about Seasonal Affective Disorder. This book provides information regarding the diagnosis for this condition as well as treatment plans available. Partial treatment focuses on using bright light therapy for the successful treatment of SAD.

Winter Blues: Seasonal Affective Disorder: What it is and how to Overcome it
Rosenthal, Norman E. 1998, 354 pp. Guildford Publications, Inc.
Information is provided on the dimentions of SAD. The book includes a self-test to help you evaluate your own level of SAD, as well as information regarding treatment of and coping with SAD.

Spina Bifida

Websites

www.fortunecity.com/millenium/plumpton/268/sb.htm
    Information on Spina Bifida

www.spinabifida.net
    Spina Bifida Web Sites

www.sbadv.org
    Spina Bifida Home Page

Resource Books

Teaching the Student with Spina Bifida
Rowley-Kelly, Fern L. (Ed) & Reigel, Donald H. (Ed). 1992, 470 pp. Paul H. Brookes.
This book explores the aspects of social, personal, and cognitive development in students with Spina Bifida.

Children with Spina Bifida: A Parent's Guide
Lutkenhof, Marlene (ed). 1999, 395 pp. Woodbine House
A very informative text for parents of special children with Spina Bifida. This book provides information in an easy-to-understand, nonfrightening, supportive way.

Children's Picture Books

Patrick and Emma Lou
Holcomb, Nan & Yoder, Dot (ill). 1992, 32 pp. Jason and Nordic Publishers.
Despite his excitement over walking with a new walker, three-year-old Patrick finds it isn't easy and becomes discouraged until his new friend, six-year-old Emma Lou who has spina bifida, helps him discover something important about himself.

Traumatic Brain Injury

Websites

www.neuroskills.com/index.html
Traumatic Brain Injury Resource Guide

www.tbiguide.com
Traumatic Brain Injury

www.tbims.org
Traumatic Brain Injury Model Systems

www.biausa.org
Brain Injury Association USA Home Page

Resource Books

Coping with Mild Traumatic Brain Injury
Stoler, Diane R. & Hill, Barbara, A. 1998, 334 pp. Avery Publishing Group, Inc.
Using clear, easy-to-understand language, the authors look at how the brain works and how it can be injured. They also discuss the procedures used to diagnose brain injuries, and the different treatments available.

Childhood Traumatic Brain Injury:
Diagnosis, Assessment and Intervention
Bigler, Erin D. (Ed); Clark, Elaine (Ed); & Farmer, Janet, E. (Ed). 1997, 342 pp. Pro-Ed.
This resource provides information regarding the diagnosis of TBI, the assessment used to determine severity of, and also effective intervention techniques to use with children with TBI.

Traumatic Brain Injury in Children and Adolescents
Tyler, Janet S. & Mira, Mary P. 1999, 149 pp. Pro-Ed, Incorporated.
A sourcebook providing information for teachers and other school personnel when working with children and adolescents with TBI.

Children with Traumatic Brain Injury
Lisa Schoenbrodt, Ed.D (Ed). 2001, 350 pp. Woodbine House.
A reference for parents that provides support and information to help their child recover from a traumatic brain injury. Not only a helpful resource for parents, but it also is useful for professionals who provide services to children with TBI and their families.

Subject Index

References

Bender, W. N. (2001). *Learning disabilities: Characteristics, identification, and teaching strategies*. (4th ed.). Boston: Allyn and Bacon.

Canter, L., & Canter M. (1997). Succeeding with difficult students. Santa Monica, CA: Lee Canter & Associates.

Clayman, C. B. (Ed.). (1989). The american medical association encyclopedia of medicine. New York: Random House, Incorporated.

Dornbush, M. P. & Pruitt, S. K. (1995). Teaching the tiger: A handbook for individuals involved in the education of students with attention deficit disorders tourette syndrome, or obsessive-compulsive disorder. Duarte, CA: Hope Press.

Dulcan, M. K. (Ed.). (1999). Helping parents, youth, and teachers understand medications for behavioral and emotional problems: A resource book of medication information handouts. Washington, DC: American Psychiatric Press.

Heward, W. L. & Orlansky, M. D. (1999). Exceptional children. (6th ed.). New York: Macmillan Publishing Company.

Kerr, M. M., & Nelson, C. M. (1997). Strategies for managing behavior problems in the classroom. (3nd ed.). New York: Macmillan Publishing Company.

Kerr, M. M., Nelson, C. M., & Lambert, D. L. (1987). Helping adolescents with learning and behavior problems. Columbus, OH: Merrill Publishing Company.

McLoughlin, J. A., & Lewis, R. B. (2000). Assessing students with special students. (5th ed.). New York: Macmillan Publishing Company.

Mercer, C. D. & Mercer, A. R. (2000) Teaching students with learning problems. (6th ed.). New York: Macmillan Publishing Company.

Minnesota Department of Children, Families & Learning. (1996). Total special education systems (TSES) generic policies and procedures manual. Little Canada, MN: Author.

Reif, S. F. (1993). How to reach and teach ADD/ADHD children. New York: The Center for Applied Research in Education.

Sugai, G. M., & Tindal, G. A. (1993). Effective school consultation: An interactive approach. Pacific Grove, CA: Brooks/Cole Publishing Company.

If you have questions, would like to place an order, or request a catalog feel free to contact us by mail, e-mail, telephone or fax.
We will be happy to assist you.

Peytral Publications, Inc.
PO Box 1162
Minnetonka, MN   55345

Toll free: 1-877-PEYTRAL (877-739-8725)
Fax: (952) 906-9777
Questions? Call (952) 949-8707

We encourage you to visit our web site for the most current listing of new titles and perennial best sellers!
www.peytral.com